# GOOD OLD DAYS
## in the

# KITCHEN

HOUSE of
WHITE

Editors: Ken and Janice Tate
Copy Editor: Läna Schurb

Production Coordinator: Brenda Gallmeyer
Creative Coordinator: Shaun Venish
Cover Design: Dan Kraner
Design/Production Artist: Becky Sarasin
Traffic Coordinator: Sandra Beres
Production Assistants: Carol Dailey, Chad Tate

Photography Manager: Vicki Macy
Photography: Tammy Christian, Nancy Sharp
Photography Assistants: Linda Quinlan, Arlou Wittwer

Publishers: Carl H. Muselman, Arthur K. Muselman
Chief Executive Officer: John Robinson
Marketing Director: Scott Moss
Editorial Director: Vivian Rothe
Production Director: George Hague

Printed in the United States of America
First Printing: 1998
Library of Congress Number: 98-73374
ISBN: 1-882138-39-2

Every effort has been made to ensure the accuracy of the material
in this book. However, the publisher is not responsible for research
errors or typographical mistakes in this publication.

*Dear Friends of the Good Old Days,*

Did you ever notice how everything seemed to be *bigger* back in the days of our youth? The pastures were bigger, the trees taller and the creeks wider and deeper.

Nothing seemed bigger to me in my young life than Mama's kitchen.

It, not the living room, was really the center of life, the nerve center of our family. There, yes, we ate our meals—but so much more. There we baked cookies, our first scientific experiments. There we kept chicks, piglets and baby kittens warm from winter's bitter cold. There we learned early responsibility, whether it was bringing a bucket of water from the spring or washing dishes for Mama. There we learned about faith as we innocently said our first prayers: "God is great; God is good. Now we thank Him for our food. Amen."

More importantly, there we learned *sharing*.

We learned sharing around the big wooden table, where we shared our thoughts, our hopes, our dreams. We shared news—and Daddy's news about the war in no way diminished my news about the new calf I had found or the turtle I had caught. We shared time, whether it was following Mama's apron strings from the pantry to the stove to the cupboard, or clearing off the table after supper for a game of cards or dominoes.

If there is one thing I think the children of today are missing above all it would have to be those hundreds of hours outside the presence of television and in the presence of love.

I hope this collection of stories from the gardens, kitchens and pantries of our youth brings you a warmth generated by memories of four-hole woodburning stoves, hot cocoa and fresh gingerbread cookies. Those memories fuel the fire as we remember the *Good Old Days in the Kitchen.*

# ❋ Contents ❋

## From the Garden • 6

## To the Kitchen • 38

## To the Table • 76

## Around the Kitchen • 130

# Chapter 1

## From The Garden

I still enjoy gardening after all these years, even if my bad back doesn't like me to put out much more than a small patch. To me there is nothing much better than a pan of green beans Janice cooks up just after we've picked, snipped and washed them. And can there be anything more heaven-sent than a ripe tomato, a shaker of salt, and a porch swing?

I know Janice and I get our love of growing good things to eat from the days when our families had to grow enough to get us through the winter. There just wasn't enough money to go to the general store for all the victuals for a family of five. Those days of need taught us not to take for granted these days of plenty.

So, whenever Janice and I bring in a hill or two of potatoes from the garden to our little country kitchen, I thank God for the abundance of food—and memories—He has blessed us with. Enjoy these tales from the garden.

—Ken Tate

# Our Apple-Peeling Parties

*By Dori Kell*

There has been many a story written about quilting bees, but in our Ohio Valley in the late 1800s and early 1900s, we had another way of socializing—apple-peeling parties.

When there was a bumper crop of apples, many of these parties were given on Saturday nights in very late fall. All families within traveling distance were invited and asked to bring a covered dish for dinner. There were so many people that the parties were held in the front part of the barn. The tables were set with pans and knives. There were never enough chairs, and many people would bring their own.

Mr. Beyer's apple parties were known to be the best and he was having one tonight. There were bushels and bushels of fresh red apples everywhere. His trees always had an abundance. They were so full of apples that the branches bent to the ground and some even cracked under the weight of the luscious fruit. The apples were so beautiful that they could have been used for advertising—picture perfect, red, large and juicy. He knew just when to spray and fertilize his trees and was an expert on fruit trees. It was no accident that his trees yielded so much more than his neighbors'.

> **Mr. Beyer's apple parties were known to be the best and he was having one tonight.**

His barn was rumored to be kept cleaner than the inside of his home. He was Pennsylvania Dutch and worked most of his waking hours. Early this morning he was hanging lanterns carefully from rafters and large nails above. He was making certain that everything was in order for tonight. He bought heavy string and large-eyed needles from the General Store yesterday. He knew he didn't have enough lanterns but just like the chairs, many would bring their own.

Large bushel baskets of delicious Rome, Baldwin, Jonathan and McIntosh apples were placed on the floor by every fourth chair. After an hour or two of peeling, there was a delicious aroma of spicy apple-buttery fragrance that couldn't be duplicated anywhere else but at one of these parties.

It would take nearly 20 baskets of fresh apples, sliced and strung, to make three baskets of dried apples for winter storage. They were dried on a large platform—Mr. Beyer's invention—in the sun. The yard long

if they liked after the work was done.

There was a lot of teasing and laughing. Everyone tried to top one another in peeling an apple with one whole strand intact. This was very hard to do and do fast. Fred Todd was the expert at this, and how he boasted, for he knew no one could beat him. Everyone tried but failed.

Near the end of the peeling, the older women left the younger ones to finish up and went to prepare the food for the scrumptious dinner that would soon be spread from one end of the barn to the other.

A barrel of apple cider was tapped for the children and pots of hot chocolate and coffee were brought in for the adults. There were large hams, skillets full of pork chops, chicken pies and steaks. Vegetables were plentiful and fixed in every conceivable way. The desserts were endless and most of them were made with—you guessed it—apples.

There was to be a contest for the best apple recipe tonight. The winner would get a new apple-peeling machine from France that had just been invented. It could peel seven apples in one minute!

There were dried-apple pies, each made in its own special way. The following happens to be my grandmother's recipe.

### Dried-Apple Pie

1½ cups boiling water
1½ cups dried apples
½ cup brown or white sugar
½ teaspoon ground cinnamon
½ teaspoon ground nutmeg
Pastry for double-crust pie
2 tablespoons butter
Pour boiling water over dried apples and let set half a day. Add sugar and spices and stir well. Line pie pan with bottom crust, then pour apple-spice mixture into this. Dot well with butter and put top crust on. Bake in fairly hot oven 45–60 minutes, or until golden brown.

strands of sliced apples were laid on the raised floor in a well ventilated area, then covered with thin muslin sheeting. They would have to be turned every two or three hours until they dried.

Most of the families started to arrive around dusk. It was a very hot and humid day and was just starting to cool down. The barn doors were kept wide open in opposite directions to catch the cool evening breeze, if and when it should start to blow.

At these parties, there were people of all ages—the elderly, the mature, the middle-aged and the young. The mature and middle-aged peeled the apples and the elderly strung them. The young people helped wherever they could, emptying peelings into a barrel for the hogs or refilling empty apple baskets. The men hung the finished strands on a line, being careful not to drop them on the earthen floor.

Just like the quilting bees and Easter sings, this was another way for the young eligible people to meet one another. They could pair off

The apples were in everything, like apple slaw, Waldorf salad, apple dumplings, apple kuchens, apple betty and baked apples with

walnuts and raisins stuffed in the center. An apple-cheese pie won the contest. It really looked and tasted superb. What an idea to combine the two! The recipe was taken home by all the women.

The young girls started to disappear to freshen up and take off their aprons. The table was almost filled to the brim by now and Mr. Beyer stood on a nail keg, clapping his hands for attention. He smiled and shouted, "Thanks, everyone, for your help," and then asked the minister for the blessing. "Eat to your heart's content, you deserve it," he groaned, mopping his forehead with his handkerchief. The food began to disappear just like the young couples who had been eyeing one another.

It was an evening of fun. Everyone talked for months about the great time they had that night. On his visits to help his neighbors weeks later, Mr. Beyer noticed without comment their platforms, just like his for drying their apples. ◆

### Stewed Apples and Rice

Peel good baking apples; take out the cores with a scoop so as not to injure the shape of the apples; put them in a deep baking dish and pour over them a syrup made by boiling sugar in the proportion of 1 pound to 1 pint of water. Put a little piece of shredded lemon inside each apple and let them bake very slowly until done, but not in the least broken.

If the syrup is thin, boil it until it is thick enough. Take out the lemon peel and put a little jam inside each apple and between them little heaps of well-boiled rice.

This dish may be served either hot or cold.

*This recipe was in an 1877 cookbook which belonged to my mother.*

*—Mrs. John A. Boller*

## Ode to Apple Pie

The bards of old, in verse have told
Of lovers bold and gay,
Of Lochinvar and his guiding star
And their dash o'er the highland brae;
Of Romeo and Othelilo
Of war and the battle cry,
Oh, let me sing of a plebian thing,
In my *Ode to Apple Pie.*
The poets tell of the binding spell
Of the villian's evil look;
Of warriors tried, who fought and died
On the banks of a babbling brook;
Of prisoners led to dungeon's dread
To pine away and die—
Oh, let me sing of a pleasanter thing,
In my *Ode to Apple Pie.*
Time takes all, both great and small,
The old bards have passed away,
And in their place stands another race—
The bards of the present day.
But still their lay is far away
From the things for which I sigh.
The tales they tell me may all be well,
But give me apple pie.
So through this life of pain and strife,
Of toil and struggle for gold,
Of changing scenes and new machines,
Of troubles, new and old.
Of the endless race to hold our place,
And to keep on "getting by"—
It wouldn't be bad, if we always had
Plenty of apple pie.
And when at last our day is past,
And we climb the golden stair,
And we look and see our reward to be
For trying to do our share,
There'll be harps and wings and
other things
And joys that never die.
And in that day, I hope and pray,
There'll be plenty of apple pie.

*—Murry G. Sawyer*

# Grandma & Green Tomatoes

*By Virginia Hearn Machir*

My grandmother was born in 1867 when Andrew Johnson was president, and died in 1944 at the age of 77 years. She was born just two years after President Lincoln was assassinated. She gave birth to five children, all of whom survived. I remember her in her last days, a plump, soft little woman with snowy hair and bright blue eyes, sitting on a cane-bottom chair in her airy kitchen during a late-summer day, as she cut up green tomatoes to make green tomato mincemeat and chowchow.

In Grandma's time, part of which I shared with her as a very young girl, the family that didn't can their food didn't eat, as there was very little store-bought food. Canning and preserving food was vital to rural life. The only store-bought foods Grandma purchased were coffee, sugar, flour and baking powder.

She canned hundreds of quarts of fruits and vegetables and stored them on shelves in the velvety darkness of the root cellar. There was row upon row of shining jars of green beans, red tomatoes, dark red beets, yellow peaches, watermelon rind preserves, pear preserves, blackberries, green tomato mincemeat, green tomato pickles, chowchow and relish. She never let one green tomato go to waste.

Late in summer before the frost, Grandma and I would go into the garden and gather all the green tomatoes. We put some of them away in the cellar to ripen, often enjoying them throughout the holiday season. Grandma liked to use some of the green ones for frying, some for mincemeat, pickles, relish, chowchow and green tomato pie.

For supper the first night we usually had fried green tomatoes. This simple but appetizing dish was tops with Grandma's family. She would slice the green tomatoes, pepper and salt them, then coat the slices well with a mixture of flour and cornmeal and fry them in hot grease until they were golden brown. They were luscious.

The next day my job was to wash the Mason jars in a large dishpan of hot, sudsy water. Then I placed the jars in a pan of boiling water to sterilize them. Grandma had hundreds of blue glass Mason and Ball jars. The other week I was at an auction and one of those old blue glass Ball Ideal jars that was dated July 14, 1908 brought $8. I wish I still had all the old blue jars from Grandma's cellar; I'd have quite a windfall.

Grandma was busy grinding green tomatoes in the food chopper to make mincemeat, relish and chowchow. She salted the ground green tomatoes, put the mixture into a flour sack and hung the bag on the clothesline to drain overnight. The next day she'd add chopped apples, chopped raisins, lemon juice, brown sugar and spices. When she put the mixture on the stove to bring it to a boil, a spicy, tangy aroma filled the entire house.

Next she ladled the mixture into the hot, sterilized jars, screwed the lids on tight and put the jars into a hot water bath to process, or "cold pack," as she said.

The pinnacle of the green tomato season arrived when Grandma baked her green tomato pie from the fresh fruit. Following is her recipe.

### Grandma's Green Tomato Pie

Pastry for 2-crust pie
3 cups sliced green tomatoes
6⅓ cups sugar
3 tablespoons flour
¼ teaspoon salt
6 tablespoons lemon juice
4 teaspoons grated lemon rind
¾ teaspoon ground cinnamon
3 tablespoons butter or margarine

Preheat oven to 450 degrees. Line pie pan with pastry.

Combine green tomatoes with sugar, flour, salt, lemon juice and rind. Pour filling into pastry-lined pan; dot with butter and cinnamon. Cover with top crust.

Bake at 450 degrees for 10 minutes; reduce heat to 350 degrees and bake 30 minutes longer, or until tomatoes are tender.

Once you cut into a green tomato pie and take a morsel into your mouth, you'll know you have tasted mouth-watering goodness.

I'm thankful for the lessons in canning green tomatoes I received from my grandmother. Sometimes of a summer evening when I'm sitting in my lawn chair daydreaming in the dusk, I can still see her in the kitchen, sitting in the old cane-bottom chair, cutting up green tomatoes. ◆

## Canning Tomatoes

On Saturday mornings, my mother
    would call
from the foot of the staircase and
    say,
"Wake up, come downstairs, help
    me wash jars;
we're canning tomatoes, today."
I grumbled and griped but finally
    came down;
the tomatoes were on the porch
    floor.
Daddy had picked them in four
    bushel baskets;
my day would be filled with the
    boring chore.
I washed Mason jars in hot, soapy
    water;
I twisted my hands way down in
    them;
I poured boiling water on those
    red, ripe tomatoes,
and then let them soak until I could
    skin them.
The peel slipped off easy, so I did
    that first,
then pared out the spidery core.
I cut up red pieces and packed them
    in jars,
and then it was time to scald more.
Measuring salt and water
    to cover,
Mama placed the filled jars in the
    canner.
She watched them with care, the
    time and the pressure,
to process them in a safe manner.
Canning tomatoes is
    one memory
that I never connected with
    pleasure,
But when I look back on my
    self-satisfaction,
those most boring moments I
    treasure.

—By Mary Virginia Rogers

# Mama's Pantry

*By Betty Artlip Lawson*

If heaven has a smell and it isn't the same as the ambrosial fragrance remembered from childhood as the one issuing forth from Mama's pantry, it cannot be a better smell, so it can only be a different one. Whenever I wished to impress a girlfriend with the fine quality of my home, a visit to the pantry was in order. That room never failed to impress each and every one. I rated the intelligence of my friends by the amount of appreciation they showed for my favorite room.

I was only 5 when we moved into the house with the pantry. It was a small room off the kitchen. The wallpaper was stained and the 3-foot-high wainscoting was chipped, stained and dirty.

One of the first jobs Mama tackled was to scrub the entire room. Then she washed the ceiling-high, glass-door cupboard which covered an entire wall of this delightful room. She polished the glass doors until they gleamed, then began to fill the cupboard. The very top shelves held her company dishes. The other higher shelves held pickling spices and three or four jars each of her home-canned fruits and vegetables. These were for current use and came from the larger store in the outdoor cave.

The lower shelf was kept for the really fine products of her baking wizardry and other cooked foodstuffs which were currently part of our menu. Some days the lowest shelf held a spicy smell of pickling, livening up the yummy pantry smell. Under the shelf on the side opposite the cupboard, there were always a few winter onions. Strange as this may sound, these only made the combined odors more pleasing.

In the fall, Mama made ketchup. A bottle or two was left lightly stoppered on one of the pantry shelves and this spicy tomato aroma was also very pleasant. Each year, we kids dug up horseradish. This was washed, ground, salted and put in a crock. It was then covered with vinegar and put in the pantry where it was allowed to "work" awhile. When it was ready, we kids packed it into small jars and peddled it from door to door. This also added to the rich-smelling atmosphere of the pantry.

Throughout the summer and fall, there would be strawberries, peaches, tomatoes, apples, green beans, apricots and all manner of lovely smelling garden and orchard produce under the shelf opposite the cupboard. These took up only temporary residence while awaiting Mama's attentions at the cookstove. They soon would be put into jars for the winter feeding of six hungry children.

*Whenever I wished to impress a girlfriend with the fine quality of my home, a visit to the pantry was in order.*

These six children had voracious appetites, but Mama was always more than equal to the challenge. When I was very young, the shortage of money surely caused her many anxious moments in regard to her ability to keep up with her healthy and forever-hungry children, but as the financial situation improved, she appeared to find her task challenging and satisfying.

Mama did not like to prepare breakfast. She taught us to provide our own at a very early age. Cereal, toast and milk was the invariable menu.

The meal called dinner was the big meal of the day and was always put on the table at noon. Children always came home from school for dinner. This meal was probably meat, potatoes and gravy, two vegetables or one vegetable and salad, followed by dessert. Supper was usually a sandwich or casserole with fruit or a light dessert, served at 6 p.m.

Because of the six hours between our second and third meals, we were always allowed a

*Continued on page 17*

# The Pecan King

*By Eve Milton Abbott*

The truth is that most people in the United States have eaten Uncle Fred's pecans and enjoyed them without ever knowing his name or how much work went into producing the best pecan in the world.

Uncle Fred loved pecans. He could hardly wait for Thanksgiving and Christmas when he was younger because that time of year always meant pecans. Pecan pies, parched, salted pecans, pecan toppings, pecans, pecans, pecans.

Young Fred was fascinated by their many shapes and colorations and differences in tastes, but one thing always pestered and aggravated him each and every time he cracked a pecan—how hard it was to get the nut out whole or even in halves. Each time he got just pieces for all of his time-consuming efforts, and he detested it.

*The Mahan Papershell Pecan won all the major awards, and Uncle Fred was crowned the "Pecan King."*

Uncle Fred was fortunate in that his family owned one of the largest nurseries of the early 1900s and so he had a good feel for the business of plant experimentation and crossbreeding. He spent years researching pecans. He would travel a thousand miles if he heard of a promising pecan, to see if it would meet his idea of what a nut should be, but to no avail.

His family learned that a small nursery in the South was in financial difficulty and sent Uncle Fred down to see about buying out their stock of plants.

Uncle Fred bought the nursery instead, and thus embarked on a dream. He immediately set about researching the pecans in the North Florida-South Georgia area.

His forays took him to Mississippi when he heard of a woman who had an unusual pecan tree on her property.

After seeing the nuts, Uncle Fred felt that he had discovered the beginning of his dream. He bought the tree and took some scions and carefully carried them home. His find would be worthless if he could not bud or graft the new wood onto his stock trees.

After months of daily observation, Uncle Fred could see that the stock tree and new wood were working together and he was satisfied that he had his "dream pecan." He was so sure of his pecan that he entered it into the World Class Competition—and it won. On making its debut in 1925, the Mahan Papershell Pecan won all the major awards, and Uncle Fred was crowned the "Pecan King."

Uncle Fred held that title for the rest of his life. His dream brought him great monetary riches, but the papershell pecan bearing his name brought him his greatest riches—the realization of a dream.

With some of the money from sales of his pecan, he did other research work and produced new marketable pecans and other fruit trees. He once said that he was so appreciative of the State of Florida for so richly providing him with so much that he wanted to repay her and her citizens.

He gave 400,000 flowering trees, greenery and shrubs to the State of Florida and used his own work crews to landscape the 26-mile stretch of State Highway 90 that led from his nursery to the capital of Florida. The highway was named the Fred Mahan Highway and is one of Florida's most beautiful roadways.

The roadsides are lovely throughout the year, just as Uncle Fred had planned when he planted crepe myrtle for long summer blooms, palm and arborvitae for greenery, holly and other shrubs and pyracanthas for winter color with their berries, and azaleas, camellias and dogwood for spring splendor.

Besides being recognized by the State of Florida, he also was written up in notable publications like *The Coronet and Who's Who.*

Today Uncle Fred lies at rest beneath large oaks surrounded by redbuds, azaleas, camellias, dogwoods and magnolias on the nursery he so loved. Although he died in the early 1960s, he lives on. Each time the city trees are ablaze with color or the state highway breaks out in glorious tints and hues, Fred Mahan is alive.

As a matter of fact, you probably used some of his pecans if you bought pecans to make a pie. Included is one of his favorite pecan recipes. ◆

### Mahan Pecan Sandies

1 cup butter
¼ cup confectioners' sugar
2 teaspoons vanilla extract
1 tablespoon water
2 cups flour
1 cup chopped Mahan pecans
Additional confectioners' sugar

Preheat oven to 300 degrees. Cream butter and confectioners' sugar until light and fluffy. Add vanilla and water and beat well.

Sift flour. Add to butter-sugar mixture. Blend well. Add nuts. Shape into small rolls about 1½ x ½ inches and place on an ungreased cookie sheet.

Bake for about 20 minutes; while still warm, roll in additional confectioners' sugar.

# *Mama's Pantry*

*Continued from page 15*

snack from the pantry when school was finished for the day. Putting our schoolbooks down as we came through the back door, we immediately checked the pantry. Because our mother was a willing baker and a very accomplished maker of pies and cake, we did not find these two fine desserts to be anything special. However, our friends did. While I mashed white beans and spread them on bread for my own peculiar gourmet sandwich delight, I invited the friend of the day to choose which pie or cake she would like. The answer was nearly always, "Oh, I better not eat those things. Your mom is probably saving them for something special."

"No, she isn't," I'd answer. "She will make more tomorrow." It never failed to impress them.

Likely because of the delicious, always-available variety of food in Mama's pantry, more than half of her six children find themselves forever fighting the battle of the bulge. But, also because of Mama's frequent lessons in common sense, none of us ever allow our weight to get completely out of control. It is about time for me to start another diet, so I wanted to get all these delicious, delectable thoughts out of my head and onto paper, so they may leave me in peace until such time as my bathroom scale and my common sense may once again allow me the luxury of remembering Mama's pantry. ◆

### Tomato Ketchup

Let 1 gallon tomato juice stand in a warm place for 4 or 5 days until it really sours.

Skim off top and part of water from top. Use tomato juice and add sugar and spice to taste, some finely ground onions, and salt. No vinegar is used.

Boil slowly until it is as thick as desired and seal.

This surely is a good recipe. I used it this past summer.

*—Mrs. Golden Pitman*

# Game Meals

*By Violet Moore*

When I think about it now, there was a reason why we children were so well acquainted with the taste and texture of wild meats, such as rabbit and squirrel. They were our everyday fare.

The time was the early '30s. The Depression with a capital "D" was being as acutely felt on the small farm as in the city, but there was nothing depressing about the food my mother managed to set on the big golden oak dining table three times a day. We had milk and eggs, and a demanding monster of a vegetable garden in which we all labored according to our ages and capabilities. Even the littlest ones weeded, picked beans and peas, and brushed potato bugs into paper bags to be burned.

*We children were so well acquainted with the taste of wild meats because they were our everyday fare.*

Beef had just about disappeared from our menu, Daisy, our faithful milk producer, was the only bovine about the place. Chickens were for egg-laying, and any hen suspected of slacking off on her job ended up as Sunday chicken pie.

Papa and the boys, Thad, 15, and Bart, 13, were avid hunters. We ate squirrel at least once a week, rabbits maybe twice. Old John, once a hired worker on the farm, always dressed the game, just as he always cleaned our fish, killed our Thanksgiving turkey, and helped with the hog butchering each winter. His pay was usually taken in kind—backbone and liver during hog killin', meal when he shelled corn and took it to the nearby mill, and a plate piled high with fried fish or rabbit, rice and gravy, black-eyed peas and corn bread, plus a quart Mason jar of buttermilk when he helped with the churning. He was called Lost John because his cabin, which we children love to visit, was on the extreme edge of our property, by the "hard road" where he could hail a driver for a lift to the crossroads store. His other chosen vocation was checkers.

Mama cooked squirrels just one way—seasoned, floured, browned in pork drippings and then steamed for an hour or so in their own gravy. With squirrel we always had grits, just as we always had rice with rabbit.

We rarely had Irish potatoes, but twice-baked sweet potatoes, oozing caramel and slathered with Daisy's butter, were a daily treat we were not then equipped to appreciate. Snap beans, butter beans cooked with a pod or two of okra, field peas or long over-cooked (but still delicious) cabbage completed a country meal that we consumed but rarely commented on. We might "take on" over a syrup custard or fried pies made from dried peaches, but for the most part Mama simply cooked the food and we simply accepted. We accepted biscuits or corn bread, or sometimes biscuits *and* corn bread, made fresh for every meal. It was a curious sort of "poverty."

Rabbit was everyday fare. She would fix fried rabbit (always Papa's favorite) or smothered rabbit or her own version of a "veal loaf" she had once tasted at an Atlanta restaurant. It was concocted of ground rabbit, ground salt pork, bread crumbs, eggs, onions and a little milk.

There was rabbit stew, in which garden vegetables such as onions, carrots, peas and potatoes made their appearance, and Brunswick stew, containing corn, tomatoes, onion and butter beans. Grandpa favored Mama's Brunswick stew above all others he sampled at political barbecues, Fourth of July celebrations or church fund-raisers. Grandpa's blood had a Salzburger strain, and from those hearty, stubborn, religious early settlers in Georgia's southernmost counties, he inherited the belief that the original Brunswick stew was Braunschweig stew, brought into being on the hunting preserves of German nobility, utilizing whatever small animals and birds represented the day's bag, and cooked in the open to the sound of accordion music and the steady gush of beer kegs.

We ate "birds," a generic term covering doves, "pa't'idges" and ducks. Shotguns were kept loaded for the sky-darkening clouds of blackbirds; brought down by the dishpanful, they elicited mutterings from Lost John who had to dress them with his sharp little whittling knife. But he shared joyfully in the blackbird pie baked in the same dishpan.

*For the most part Mama simply cooked the food and we simply accepted. It was a curious sort of "poverty."*

However, there was one "swamp critter" that Mama had never cooked and we had never eaten, even though we captured it regularly on hunts with our faithful hounds. That was Br'er Possum.

In the early winter when the persimmons were sweetened by frost, the possums were fat and sassy. We would set out, Bart, Thad and I (this was something country girls enjoyed too) to "tree" a possum. We had learned early that if we could get close enough to this wily marsupial to thump him with a broken limb, he would "sull," that is fake a sort of coma, and we could pick him up and pop him quickly into our croker sack (gunnysack to those north of the Mason-Dixon line). We rarely got all the way home with our squirming sack. Some plowman or fence mender would buy him from us for a dime or 15 cents, big money in those days.

It always irked Lost John when we told him what we had done with our possum. He regarded possum as the supreme forest delicacy, especially when surrounded by roasted sweet potatoes. A possum's appearance, with his sparse and grizzled hair, ropelike tail, and pointed, grinning face, is not prepossessing. He does not look like anything anyone would want to eat, an "impossumbility," so to speak. But so eloquent and wistful was Lost John that, when we next went possum hunting, we saw our prey in a new light and brought him dutifully to our old retainer's doorstep.

Now, a mother who does not balk at cooking a mess of frog legs or a neighbor's gift of chit'lin's, who can be persuaded to fry battered squash blossoms in the spring before her garden "makes," and who conspires to serve eel to a finicky aunt from town, is not going to back off from fixing possum 'n' taters to please her children.

Old John killed our fine, fat possum. John made a fire under the big, black iron pot and we pumped enough water to fill it three-quarters full. When he had scalded the animal he proceeded to pull off the hair, scraping vigorously with his all-purpose knife, and cut off the tail, feet and head. The possum was put to soak overnight in heavily salted cold water. The next day Mama drained away the salted water and put our prize on to simmer in fresh water in the big graniteware preserving kettle.

To my knowledge Mama had never attempted to cook a possum before, but she knew by prodding with her ancient two-tined kitchen fork just when it was tender enough to stop simmering and begin baking. It almost exactly filled the mottled-blue enamel roaster. Grandpa argued for a corn-bread dressing, savory with onion and dried sage, stuffed into the body cavity. Mama agreed to make dressing but felt that the half-baked sweet potatoes that had been using up the oven heat, split in half, basted with drippings and liberally peppered,

would be embellishment enough in the pan with the possum.

The range was stoked with slow-burning wood, and into the dark oven went Br'er Possum to brown like a suckling pig, the tender skin turning into cracklings as it hissed and sizzled under frequent bastings.

A small pork roast was nestled into one corner of the oven, along with the promised loaf pan of dressing. Mama had promised to bring barbecue for sandwiches to an upcoming church supper.

We children could hardly wait. We had been warned away from the small kitchen a dozen times, and finally, after our older sister had set the table and Papa had sharpened the antler-handled carving knife, the call came, "Come on, y'all! Suppertime!"

We passed our plates to Papa, one by one, and on them he piled judicious amounts of possum, dressing, sweet potatoes, black-eyed peas, egg bread, piccalilli and a small helping of the pork roast which our mother had decided to put on the table after all, since Aunt Mable was having supper with us.

The blessing over, Thad and Bart picked up their forks and I picked up mine. Thad took a mouthful of dressing, Bart of peas. I chose sweet potato.

The possum, we all agreed, looked delectable. Under Papa's quizzical glance we each raised a morsel of the meat to our lips, chewed it and chewed it and chewed it—and chewed it some more. It was the swallowing that presented difficulties.

Somehow those well-masticated mouthfuls of possum never got beyond our back teeth. We tucked them away into our cheeks as squirrels do with nuts; we disposed of them into our fists and thence into our pockets; we hid shreds of possum under the other edibles on our plate,

and gobbled up the roast pork which, strange to say, had exactly the same taste.

Mama, Papa and Aunt Mable had not helped themselves to the "varmint," as Papa persisted in calling our *pièce de resistance.* Grandpa was the sole consumer, enjoying every bite. No one scolded or ridiculed us or reminded us of the trouble Mama had taken, but I did think I heard immoderate laughter coming from my parents' room that night after we children had gone to bed.

Lost John got his liberal share of possum 'n' taters. The next night Bart, Thad and I had barbecue sandwiches at home while our parents, aunt and grandfather carried an ample supply to the church supper.

Years later, at a family reunion, Bart related the possum 'n' taters yarn for the entertainment of a fresh crop of children, town children who had never been hunting or seen a potato bug.

"It was good, real good tasting," mused Bart, "but I just couldn't swallow that possum meat.

And I never have, not to this very day."

Then Mama, frail and chair-bound but with an echo of long-ago mischief in her voice, inquired gently, "Not even possum barbecue sandwiches, son?" ◆

### Pressed Veal

Cook a shank of veal until very tender, so that the meat can be easily picked to pieces. Let the water cook down until about 1 cup of liquid remains.

Pick the veal apart; season with salt, pepper and sage. Pour the liquid from the vessel in which the meat was cooked over this. Mix thoroughly and pack closely in a pan of proper shape to make nice slices when the meat is cold. The bottom of the mold may be decorated with slices of hard-cooked eggs before the veal is put in. When set, cut thin slices and serve.

—*Ada Sheets*

# Kraut Time

*By Mabel Baldwin Couch*

In 1905 people depended on their own efforts to keep the pantry, cellar and the potato bin filled with food to satisfy the most demanding appetites.

We always raised a garden—or I should say, Mother did. It seems Mother did a great many things that this generation wouldn't know how to even begin.

In the fall, she got out the canning jars to fill with apples, plums, pumpkin and jelly. These were canned and added to the store of beets, pickles of several kinds, and relishes galore. The potatoes were in the bin, and the onions were tied and hung from rafters.

*It seems Mother did a great many things that this generation wouldn't know how to even begin.*

Fall also heralded the time for making kraut. That had been a very good year for cabbages. Plenty of rain and rich soil had produced a bumper crop. Father said, "We will leave the cabbage in the patch as long as possible. Kraut keeps better when the weather is cool." But warm rain started a second growth and those cabbages started bursting open, so kraut making had to begin.

Mother said, "We need a large jar or keg." Daddy scoured the country, but couldn't find either. Everyone seemed to be making kraut. They couldn't let all that cabbage go to waste, and could only sell it for a cent a pound. Finally, in desperation, Daddy bought a 50-gallon barrel. Mother laughed and said, "Ed, that won't do. No family would use that much kraut. Besides, we don't have enough cabbage to make it a third full. Besides—where would we put the barrel?"

Father studied a moment, then measured the space behind one door in our combination living room - bedroom, and announced, "It will set right here."

Our house consisted of only two large rooms. There were four in our immediate family, and an uncle lived with us. People lived in much smaller homes in those days. They didn't have refrigerators, electric fans, built-in ovens, and many appliances we think we "must have" in order to live today.

Mother was skeptical of kraut in a barrel, and behind the door was almost too much to consider. She looked Daddy in the eye, saying, "Do you remember what kraut smells like when it's fermenting?"

"Yes, I know it smells like heck, but we'll get used to it." I don't know how we could have lived with it, but somehow we did.

The barrel was scrubbed, cleaned and rinsed until it was clean. Then it was placed behind the door.

The next morning Daddy and Uncle Jim hitched a team to the wagon and went for the cabbage. Two neighbors who didn't aim to make kraut laughingly told Daddy, "Ed, since you're going to make a barrel, you might just as well take our cabbage, too." Altogether, they had a fair load of cabbage.

Early next morning the work began. Mother had an old-fashioned kraut cutter with two blades and a "box" that held the cabbage as she slid it up and down, slicing the cabbage into a big dishpan. They worked hard for about three hours and the bottom of the barrel was scarcely more than covered.

Daddy said, "I think I know a better way than this."

Following a discussion, he went to town, and returned with a brand-new sharpshooter. Mother washed and scalded it well.

They changed their procedure. Mother and Uncle Jim cleaned and trimmed the cabbages my brother and I carried to them after we had removed the rotten, dirty and worm-eaten leaves. They cored the cabbage and cut it in quarters and tossed it into the barrel. Daddy was vigorously chopping, chopping, chopping, chopping. Noon came, with quick lunch and a short rest period—then back to work.

They had been adding a handful of salt with

the quartered cabbage once in awhile. Mother assured the men, "The proper way is to weigh 5 pounds of cabbage and add 4 tablespoons of salt." But after they weighed the cabbage four times using the hand scales, the men decided "guessing" would do just as well as so much measuring, so "by guess" is the way that kraut was made. Believe me, their guesses must have been very nearly correct, for that was the best kraut I've ever eaten.

After it was chopped, Mother took two large sand rocks and scrubbed and scalded them for weights to hold the kraut down.

First she put clean 100-pound flour sacks over it. Then the rocks were put on, and the cabbage juice well nigh covered the rocks. Then other flour sacks were stretched over the barrel and tied down.

Once a week Mother took the rocks out and carefully removed the sacks, taking the scum out also. Sacks and rocks were washed and scalded and replaced. This went on for several weeks. So did the horrible smell—but patience is a virtue. Finally, they decided the cabbage was "kraut." I'd love to have a mess of kraut today as good as that kraut was—crisp, juicy and with the very best flavor. We ate kraut and divided with neighbors until, when spring came, the kraut barrel was empty.

The good Lord must have blessed their efforts. Now people can kraut in quart or half-gallon jars, and sometimes it spoils. I reckon germs are much more plentiful now. No one would dream of cutting it with a sharpshooter, mauling it with a kraut stamper to pack it close, weighting it down with rocks, and living to eat a half-barrel of kraut. ◆

# When Grandpa Made Apple Butter

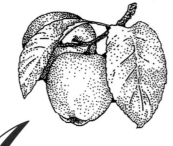

*By Zenobia Thomas*

As I look back, it seems as if all the magic spices of the Indies could not conjure up the aroma that arose from the final simmering of the deep, dark burgundy apple butter as it bubbled in the big iron kettle which squatted over the slow-burning fire in the yard behind the old house at Grandpa's. It took hours to cook the apple butter to the epitome of its goodness. It took a lot of work, too, but that work always seemed lighter when it became the project of many members of the family who helped bring it to its final stage of mouth-watering deliciousness.

During my childhood, when my mother, brother and I lived with my grandfather, certain days always stood out as special because they called for collective effort on the part of many. For instance, when Grandpa made apple butter, aunts of whom I was fond and cousins whom I liked and admired always came to help get everything ready for making the delectable spread.

*Grandpa fondly believed, after Grandma died, that he was the only one who really knew how to make apple butter in just the right way.*

I say "when Grandpa made the apple butter" because he fondly believed, after Grandma died, that he was the only one who really knew how to do it in just the right way. Maybe he was, because everyone else went along with it and let him attend to all of the cooking and seasoning of the apples. My uncles helped him only when he requested it or when there were apples to be carried from one place to another. My aunts, cousins, mother and I got the apples ready for him.

Like many farms at that time, where many of the raw materials needed to furnish the food then considered necessary were home-grown, there was a good-sized apple orchard near the house. While I no longer remember all of the kinds of apples which grew in the orchard, I do remember that during the summer, apple butter was made from the transparent apples before they became too ripe and mealy. In my opinion, those apples still make the best applesauce, so it should follow that apple butter made from them had to be special, and it was! When Grandpa deemed that the transparent apples were at the right stage of maturity, a day was set aside when everyone could come and help prepare the apples for their supreme moment.

We always placed our chairs in a semicircle around a table out in the back yard where we could see Grandpa or anyone else whom he might occasionally delegate to help him when things got too tiring or difficult.

How we worked—at least my mother and my two aunts did! I remember we had a contraption, hopefully called an apple peeler, but it never proved to be very satisfactory. It was more difficult to peel an apple correctly with it than it was to peel two or three by hand. If some willing, capable person was able to get the apple positioned just right, start the crank smoothly and then keep it turning at the right speed, that apple peeler could probably skin two apples while I peeled as many. However, I always tried to add my dubious help, along with two slightly older cousins whose performances weren't much better than mine because they were usually more interested in exchanging their teen-age confidences with each other than in filling their pails with peeled apples.

After the apples were peeled, quartered and cored, they were carefully washed at the well pump which was pumped by the windmill if there was enough breeze, or by hand if there wasn't. Then the apples were carried out to Grandpa by one of my uncles—or by my brother, who had to take part in the preparation if he couldn't manage to be elsewhere. Fresh apples were added, a pailful or two at a time, on top of the partially cooked apples which already had been placed in the big, black kettle.

It took almost constant stirring, the right amount of cider, cinnamon, nutmeg and other spices Grandpa felt were necessary for his own special brand of apple butter. I never did know all of the ingredients he added, but my aunts often accused him of adding another more potent liquid besides fresh cider, because it did seem to have a special taste that other apple-butter makers couldn't quite duplicate. To add to their suspicions, he never liked anyone

staying around him too long while he cooked the apples. However, they didn't pry too much, probably because the apple butter was so good, and they preferred not to know what the secret ingredient was for fear that they'd have to object to it on principle.

As the apples on the bottom cooked and more and more uncooked apples were added, the stirring became more difficult. Then and only then would Grandpa allow someone to relieve him for a short time so that he could rest and move around a little. He always returned to his work before very long, however, for he wouldn't trust anyone else to cook the apple butter to just the right flavor and consistency.

After the apple butter was finally cooked to perfection, most of it was ladled out into small, brown, stoneware jars which were sealed and transported to the cellar. There was always plenty left out for everyone's immediate consumption. The taste of the warm, spicy-sweet, red-brown apple butter is the part that I remember best. Never would it taste better than it did on that first day when we all sampled it and pronounced it the best ever!

Most of these apple-butter-making days were pretty uneventful. The women sat around, gossiping about who had done this or about someone who had said that as they worked at getting the apples ready for the kettle.

However, there was one day which provided us with a little excitement. On this particular day, one of my aunts and a cousin were busy peeling apples under the catalpa trees. Mother and I were at the well, where she was washing the apples and I was pumping the water into the pails for her. Perhaps I heard some unusual noise, for I looked up in time to see Grandpa performing some odd gymnastics, jumping around, slapping his leg with his hat, acting like he was trying to do an Indian war dance by the fire. As I let go of the pump handle, Mother

*It took a lot of work to make apple butter, but the work always seemed lighter when it became the project of many family members.*

looked up and followed my gaze. We saw my aunt and cousin dump their pans of apples and start running out to the old yard where Grandpa was yelling and stomping. They had to stop and open the gate, so they arrived at the old house just as my uncle came hurrying out, carrying a big basket of apples.

Concerned about the yelling, and surprised at the sight of the women rushing toward him, my uncle stepped back quickly and caught his foot on the rickety doorstep. Losing his balance, he let go of the basket to catch himself. As he did so, his weight knocked the basket forward just in time for my aunt and cousin to reach the spilled apples rolling in all directions in their path. Such slipping and hopping and kicking I had never seen and have not seen since!

Although half-frightened by Grandpa's antics and the few salty words we were able to catch, I couldn't have stopped howling with laughter if I had tried. Mother had to snort to keep from laughing aloud as we both ran to the scene, but we were unfortunate (or so I thought) in arriving too late and missing a real ringside view of the action.

By the time we got there the others had reached Grandpa, who had quit his stomping but was still slapping his out-of-shape hat against his pants leg. As he looked up to answer the excited questions everyone was throwing at him, even I could see the sheepish look on his face as he realized the commotion he had caused.

It seemed that in his concentration on putting some especially spiced cider into the kettle and mixing it well, he had stepped too close and stood too long by the fire without realizing it until he felt his leg getting very hot. When he looked down, he saw his pants cuff was on fire. Fortunately, he was wearing his old straw hat, and he used it to beat out the flames. Luckily, Grandpa wasn't burned (just burned up at his own carelessness). His heavy work socks had prevented the flames from penetrating to his leg before he was able to smother them.

Grandpa didn't tell us until later that he very nearly upset the kettle when he jerked back so suddenly. Almost tripping on one of the tripods which held the ends of the rod on which the big kettle hung, he had pushed it a little to one side. A fraction of an inch more and it would have gone down, no doubt taking a kettle two-thirds full of apple butter with it. It was a day of near-disasters!

Determining that Grandpa wasn't really hurt, we returned to our work, but for the rest of the day, every now and then, someone would let out a snicker when she thought of the scene that had been played before us. The ones who weren't there always regretted missing the action.

Such was the labor involved in making apple butter when I was a child, but it was really a labor of love. We enjoyed being together and the finished product seemed well worth the work that was put into it. I have never tasted apple butter which could compare with that which Grandpa made! ◆

# Mama & the Horseradish

*By Mary Fran Readinger*

Mama was not a woman given to easy tears, but there was one day every year at the end of winter when she could be depended upon to weep copiously. Invariably it followed a little foray made by Papa.

Choosing a day when he figured the frost was pretty well out of the ground, he armed himself with a spade and old pail and headed for the far end of the garden. On the north sided of the old log chicken house was a corner never turned by the plow. This was the site of Papa's operations.

When he returned to the house awhile later, his bucket was filled with the long, pale, earth-encrusted roots of horseradish. Thriftily he had lopped the top off each root and replanted it, insuring a crop for another spring.

It was Mama's job to make Papa's haul edible, which process was the cause of her tears. She never balked at the task, but she did insist on her own time, place and method.

Choosing a good, windy day, she would direct Papa to drag the old plank wash bench out into the dooryard and screw the hand-cranked sausage grinder onto it. Then, with the pan of scrubbed roots within reach and a cloth tied over her nose and mouth, she sat down with her back to the wind and began operations.

Some fussy folks insisted that grating the roots produced a finer-textured result, but Mama was all for getting the job done as speedily as possible. Even so, she went around with red nose and swollen eyes for a couple of days afterward.

Once it was ground, preparing the condiment was easy. To each cupful of ground root she added about a pint of cold cider vinegar in which had been dissolved half a teaspoon of salt and a couple of tablespoons of sugar. The entire mixture was stirred well, bottled and stored in a cool place for future use.

Some folks dig the roots in late summer and prepare them for winter use. I don't recall we ever did that, probably because Mama's bottles and jars were all filled with the sauces, relishes and pickles she had been so busy putting up all fall. However, by the end of winter, most of those containers were empty. Also, the level of the kraut in the 20-gallon crock was mighty low, the apple barrel nearly empty, and the root cellar ditto, except for potatoes. Fresh fruits and vegetables were not available in our small town store those days, and it was still too early to go hunting wild greens, all of which probably explains why we were so eager for a taste of that pungent member of the nasturtium family.

For a couple weeks we ate it on almost everything except pie, cake and pudding. We ate it for breakfast on fried eggs and for supper on fried potatoes. We slathered it on boiled beef and roast pork for dinner, and zipped up the dressing for Sunday night's potato salad. We perked up the last of winter weary creamed cabbage. My brother and I even "doctored" the detestable codfish Mama perforce served twice weekly during Lent. In fact, we all ate so much that Mama had to hide a couple of jars lest there be none left to accompany the Easter ham.

Nowadays, prepared horseradish can be purchased in practically every grocery store, but in my estimation, this pallid product is far inferior to the taste-teasing, tongue-tingling condiment that Mama so tearfully prepared every spring. ◆

# Oh, How I Remember

*By Frances Wolfe Haight*

My grandfather, Wilmer Wilson Wolfe, was born in Jefferson County, Pa., in 1877. His parents were of Pennsylvania Dutch and Indian descent. He was taught early in life to work hard but to enjoy it.

At age 25, he married Jennie Elizabeth Shirey, age 14. They had seven children, one of whom died of pneumonia at an early age. They lived in several small towns and finally settled in Mount Jewett, Pa., where Grandpa worked at a local glass factory until its close. Then he got a job with the Baltimore and Ohio Railroad. He worked there for nearly 20 years.

He supplied the family with wild meat the year around. My grandma baked and canned, and together they planted a big garden every spring. Grandma made as many of the family's clothes as possible, many of them sewn from printed feed sacks. She knitted all the mittens and they lasted many times longer than the ones from the stores.

**When my mother died and my father remarried, my grandparents took me to their hearts and house.**

These two hardworking people were my foster parents. When my mother died and my father remarried, my grandparents took me to their hearts and house. I remember helping to weed the garden and trying to carry buckets of coal when I was quite young. Also, I learned to use a sickle to cut tall grass and to do errands for the neighbors without expecting any pay, but I was very happy to receive a few pennies to buy candy.

I remember that Grandma always had fresh chocolate cake and ginger cookies in the kitchen. I remember the smell of homemade bread, freshly starched curtains, fried fish, gun-cleaning oil, and cough syrup made from cherry bark and different roots and herbs.

I remember the sounds of the wringer washer and the sadirons every Monday, the beating of rugs and the scythe mowing through the high grass. I remember the outhouse very well, as someone had to walk with me down the path at night.

When I was 8 years old, Grandma won the "bank night" award at the local movie theater. She used the money to have a bathroom installed and we thought we were in the lap of luxury.

I remember her plucking chickens, rolling out homemade noodles, and scrubbing the porch with leftover wash water every week. I helped do what I could but mostly just watched. Grandma was always afraid that I would hurt myself or be wasteful or break something, but she was always glad to let me watch.

We had a cow named Bossy 'til I was about 5 years old. She kicked Grandpa when he milked her so they sold her. The milk from Danielson's Dairy was almost as good as Bossy's milk. We had an icebox, but in the winter the milk was left outside under the porch. Sometimes the cream would be frozen 2 inches out of the bottle.

Nearly every Sunday and every holiday, lots of relatives would come to visit. The meal was usually chicken with noodles, gravy, biscuits, and always homemade apple or pumpkin pie for dessert. This seemed to be the favorite Sunday dinner for many people, and even when we went visiting, that was the meal served.

I remember Grandma grinding coffee in a hand-turned grinder with a small drawer. In later years Grandpa used this to grind up his homemade snuff.

With the icebox we had, we waited for the iceman to come around on regular visits. Wherever he stopped, the moment he took a chunk of ice into a house, every kid in the neighborhood ran for the truck for a small piece of ice to suck on. He always yelled at us, but I think he did it just to let us think we got away with something, because he couldn't use those small pieces anyway. I'll never forget the first people in the neighborhood with an electric refrigerator. They gave all the neighborhood kids *free* ice cubes made in the little freezer. We all thought that was just great!

We had a potbellied coal stove in the living room. The garbage and even tin cans were burned up in this stove. Ashes were strewn on the side road in winter to help prevent cars from sliding on the ice. Before the bathroom was installed, Saturday night was bath night in a big, old washtub by the stove.

When I was really young, the kitchen had a gaslight for which egg-shaped mantles could be bought at a cost of 5 cents each. Grandma got very upset if one of these got broken and she had to buy more. Our cookstove was big and black, with a place to put wood to burn and a warming oven up above.

Grandpa managed to bag a deer every hunting season. I would watch while he skinned it and prepared the meat. We set a meat grinder across two chairs. I would sit on one end and Grandpa on the other while he ground up meat for sausage which Grandma would can in quart jars.

Then, during the winter, we would have the sausage with pancakes for breakfast every morning. Ummm, good!

I have tried to teach my seven children the love, compassion and respect my grandparents taught me. In this fast, ever-changing world, children do not understand the simple pleasures we enjoyed or many of our values, and they are really missing a lot. ◆

### Radio Pudding

*Sometime in the early 1930s, before the Rural Electrical Association came through rural northern Iowa, we had a battery-operated radio. My mother heard a recipe for a dessert on the radio and copied it down, but she missed the name. So she called it Radio Pudding. It's simple to make and I still make it for my family and request it when I visit my mother.*

¾ cup brown sugar
2 cups boiling water
2 tablespoons margarine
¾ cup granulated sugar
1 cup flour
4 teaspoons baking powder
½ cup milk
1 cup raisins
Preheat oven to 350 degrees.

Combine brown sugar, boiling water and margarine in a 9 x 13-inch baking pan.

Combine sugar, flour, baking powder, milk and raisins; pour over mixture in pan without stirring.

Bake until brown, for about 30 minutes. Serve warm or cold, with ice cream or whipped cream.

—*Bonna L. Thompson*

# Gathering Greens

*By Mari Harries*

During my growing-up years in southern Missouri back in the '30s and '40s, we lived a semi-rural life in the little town of Chaffee. Though mother worked in a factory where they made men's pants, she never had forgotten her childhood close to the land. So in the spring, Mama would begin to feel the sap rising—as though she were related to the trees of the woods—and develop a "yen" for a "nice mess of greens."

The first bright, crisp, sunny Saturday morning that brought the wind in from the south, she would haul out the coats, sweaters, scarves and old "walking" shoes. Once we were safely bundled up against the chill, she and I would be off. We could smell the earth and the water and the incredible sweet freshness of new grass, leaves and shoots of plants on the wind.

Mama and I each carried a big brown paper bag, and Mama had a paring knife in her sweater pocket. Often one of Mama's lady friends would go with us. I liked that, for it meant that other kids would come along. We would talk and sing as we ambled along, watching for the familiar plants to go into our brown bags.

We would find dock plants, often called sour dock. Always there were lots of dandelions, and every leaf of that went into our bags along with lamb's-quarter, which we usually found along the railroad tracks.

We knew where there was a springhouse long since fallen into disuse where we could find wild mint. This was picked and kept separate to be added to our pot of hot tea upon return home. Then we'd also enjoy a special treat, shortbread cookies, as we sat and "rested a spell" from our labors.

In most of the fields we found wild mustard and wild onions that gave wonderful flavor, unmatched by tame garden mustard or dried onions.

Farmers then were prone to wide swings at the corners of the fields, and were unconcerned about weeds and wild plants growing near their crops. In these fallow spaces we found, among others, an occasional stand of pokeweed.

Mama was always very careful with pokeweed, because certain parts were poisonous. She picked only the smallest, newest leaves with no hint of reddish tinge. Usually she would also dig up a small section of the poke root to take home and clean and dry before storing it safely away in a labeled glass jar. Then, during the spring and summer, if anyone got poison oak with its small, runny, itchy sores, Mama took down the root, cut off a section, and boiled it. This produced a wash which she used to bathe the sores. After it was used, the wash was thrown out at once to soak into the ground immediately, for it was poisonous if drunk.

Believe me, when Mama put that wash on my sores, I danced a jig. I felt like a hot coal had been dropped on my skin. But after about two applications, there were no more sores. And I never had any scars.

My favorite green was the wild sorrel we called sheep's sorrel. Mama and I never did get a lot of this into the big brown bags because we both loved to eat it on the spot. Back then we didn't have to worry about pesticides. To this day, after 35 years, when I close my eyes I can still recall exactly the sharp, fresh, tangy taste of sheep's sorrel.

On our way home, if we found Johnny-jump-ups (wood violets) we counted that a very lucky day. We would take them home to go into a tiny glass in the center of the supper table.

After a cup of hot tea flavored with fresh mint, we got down to the real work. The tedious chore was "looking" the greens for bugs and dirt and brown spots. Then we washed them over and over until our hands got wrinkled from being in the water so long.

The reward, however, was worth the work. That night we would sit down to fresh greens cooked in clean, clear well water, and garnished with bits of crispy fried bacon. Mashed potatoes crowned with rich, hearty gravy, made in the pan where the bacon had cooked, and hot corn bread running with fresh, golden butter rounded out a meal fit for a king. There was always cold buttermilk to drink, and dessert was peach cobbler, swimming in fresh cream, and made from Mama's home-canned peaches. A friend once remarked, "You waddle away from Miz Eddy's table."

After evening prayers, I would lie in my bed and watch the stars twinkle on each side of the far-flung gauzy veil of the Milky Way. The spring wind would lash around the corner near

the head of my bed, hurrying up more rain to keep the land lush and clean. Snuggled under Mama's handmade quilts, I would go to sleep to dream about next week's expedition to "gather greens." ◆

### Dandelion Jelly

Pick 1 quart of fresh dandelion blossoms. **Note:** *Take care to avoid any that might have been exposed to herbicides, pesticides, fertilizers, etc.* Quickly rinse blossoms with cool water to remove any insects. Snip off green collars.

Combine cleaned blossoms in a saucepan with 2 quarts cold water. Bring to a boil and boil for 3 minutes. Set aside to cool.

Strain liquid, pressing petals with fingers to extract juice.

Measure 3 cups dandelion liquid into a saucepan; add 2 tablespoons lemon juice and 1 package (1¾ ounces) Sure Jell. Bring to a boil.

Add 5½ cups sugar, stirring well. Boil for 2½ minutes, stirring well. Put in jars and seal.

—*Mrs. Charles B. Reeves*

# Wild Gardens & Memories

## By O.J. Robertson

When the sun grows warm and the long-slumbering earth wakes with green wild plants, I remember my mother and the times she and I gathered wild greens. In early morning, she would say, "The blue thistles I saw peeping through the grass in the lower orchard are ready to pick, son. Would you like a mess of wild greens for dinner?"

"Oh fine," I'd reply, not that I found wild greens so tasty, but the first trek over the fields in the springtime was a treat to my winter-bound senses, with the pleasant smell of fresh-plowed earth, the sound of birds and brook, and the feel of wind in my face.

Mother would gather a tin pail, a large case knife for herself and a smaller one for me. She would put on her flowered gingham bonnet and I'd jerk on my worn winter cap. We were off to the lower orchard.

The blue thistles were green and tender, just right for picking. Mother would stick her knife under the plant and cut off its roots. Then she'd lift it and snip off the curly, dark green leaves. I'd do the same, except my leaves were usually accompanied by bits of dry grass which Mother would finger out.

"Enough thistles," she would soon say. "Let's look for wild lettuce and white blossom. Wild greens taste much better if you have different kinds in the pot." A few bunches of these and off we'd go, this time looking for lamb's-quarter, field cress and spikes of poke. Soon the pail was full and Mother would say, "We'd better get back to the house and wash our pick."

I carried water from the spring and poured it into a large wooden tub. Mom dumped the greens into the water and sloshed them about. She would pick up a handful of dripping leaves, shake them, and put them into a large pan. When all the greens were out of the tub, I'd carry more water for another wash. "I think maybe I'll cook them outside," Mom said, "Food cooked in the open has a different taste from that cooked on the kitchen stove. Run to the wood yard and bring some chips for a fire."

While I gathered kindling, Mother pressed the greens into a large black kettle which was hung on the triangular poles where we'd boiled last year's summer washings. Dry wood was piled around the kettle and a fire was started.

"My, don't they smell good!" Mother would say. "You watch the greens while I get some housework done. Keep the fire going, and don't let the pot boil dry." After awhile, Mother came out and lifted the kettle from the hook to drain off the water.

"Always parboil wild greens," Mother would explain. "My granny taught me that long ago. They don't taste so strong when you parboil them." Then she would add more water, sprinkle in some salt and dip in several tablespoons of grease for seasoning. Soon the greens were boiling again.

"Bring them in now," Mother would say when she thought they were almost done. "They can finish cooking on the stove."

The wild greens were usually served with a round pone of corn bread. "New greens, especially wild ones, are like tonic," Mom would remark as we sat down to eat. "Perks up your blood. So eat plenty, son, and you'll be as frisky as a young colt."

Few people pick wild greens anymore. I do, but only in my memory. When the late snows melt and the earth warms up and things begin to grow, I skip off to the lower orchard. Mother isn't far behind with her tin pail and sharp knife. May the wild greens always grow. ◆

# The Strawberry Festival

*By Helen Colwell Oakley*

"Grandma! Grandma! Come quick as you can!" I hollered, as I raced into the old country kitchen.

"Heavens, child. What's the matter? Are you hurt, or something?" Gram asked.

"No, but I just found a patch of the biggest, reddest, sweetest, juicy strawberries that I've ever seen—growing in the woods, right on our

property, too, honest, Gram. Let's go get them right now, before someone gets to them and takes every one of them," I pleaded.

She said, "Now, Helen, we'll have lunch; then we'll hurry right over to the woods, soon's everything's cleared away. Stop worrying. We'll get there soon enough."

That lunch was the longest lunch I ever ate, and the cleaning up afterward took so long that I thought we would never get to go strawberrying. Just when I couldn't stand the waiting any longer, Gram came around the corner of the farmhouse wearing a big-brimmed straw hat and carrying two tin pails, one for her and one for me.

I was 8 years old and spending a few weeks' vacation with Gram and Gramps Coy on their farm in Friendsville, Pa. In back of the barn was a woodland with tall, spreading trees and a winding creek. I had been gathering wildflowers when I came upon the bed of wild strawberries. I lost no time in getting back to the house to fetch Gram to the strawberry patch, and now here we were, all set to do some strawberryin'. Gram was a good scout, but she was like most of the grown-ups—never got all excited about desserts, fireworks, going swimming and things like that. But anyway, here we were, all set to fill our pails with fresh, wild strawberries that were going to mount up fast, as Gram said that they were the largest wild ones she had ever seen.

"Aren't you glad I found them, Gram?" I asked.

She had a big smile and tasted one every now and then, so I could tell she was pleased as could be.

The sun was hotter than the dickens in the woods, but the trees were shading a patch of strawberries so that it wasn't too bad, so we picked until our pails were almost full. Gram helped me catch up with her, as my pail was filling up rather slowly. I sampled just about every other one and did lots of talking as I picked. Gram said that I was just like most kids—jabbered all the time. She was always nice to her grandchildren, though, and most always listened to what they had to say and took the time to answer their never-ending questions.

After the pails were full, Gram wanted to sit down by the little stream nearby to catch her breath and rest for a spell before heading back for the house.

"Gram, can I take off my shoes and socks and wade in the creek?" I begged.

"For a few minutes, but only a very few, as we have to take these berries into the pantry where it will be cool for them. Then I shall make us a strawberry shortcake if you will help me look them over and hull them," said Gram.

Golly, gee! This was such a good day— finding those luscious strawberries and going wadin', all in one day. The water was cool— how can water in the creeks be cool when it is a scorching hot day? I shivered as I waded where the water came up to my knees.

"Come, Helen, it's time to start back. The sun is going down and we've got lots to do!" I didn't have a towel to dry my wet feet, so she gave me her large apron; her aprons sure came in handy at times! I had to carry the apron all rolled up in a ball to the hamper in the farm bathroom and Gram carried the pails of strawberries into the pantry.

The strawberries were so plump and pretty when we got them all hulled. Gram filled a large bowl with berries, adding a little sugar and stirring gently. Then she baked a large, square pan of shortcake; it was raised up high and nice and brown on the top. When it had cooled, she cut it into large squares.

After our supper of meat, potatoes and vegetables, Gram announced that we had a surprise for dessert. Out from the pantry came dishes of strawberry shortcake with the bright red berries oozing out between the slices, on the top, and filling the sauce dish, and to top it all off, there was a huge splash of whipped cream. Was I ever proud when Gram said that I was the one to thank for dessert, as I was the one who found the berries. Gram made the best strawberry shortcake in the whole wide world.

It was a baking-powder biscuit dough, and then she buttered the slices as the pieces were slit, just before the berries were added.

That night I had a beautiful dream all about strawberries. There I was in "strawberry land," picking berries with a strawberry princess, and living in Gram's house that had strawberry pink siding and a whipped cream roof. The next morning I told Gram all about my dream in "strawberry land." She laughed, then asked, "How would you like to go to a real strawberry festival? There's one at Forest Lake on Sunday afternoon."

I wondered what a strawberry festival was. Does everyone search for strawberries in the fields, or sell strawberries in little baskets, hull strawberries, or bake strawberry shortcakes?

Sunday turned out to be a gorgeous day, with sunshine and soft breezes, fluttering the lace curtains in the farmhouse. There had been a rain in the night. Gram said that the strawberry festival would be called off if there was rain, but now the rain was gone and the sun would soon dry the lawns and walks. We dressed in our church clothes in the afternoon and started out for the strawberry festival. Riding in Grandfather's car was fun on the country roads, just like riding in a roller coaster. He would tear down the hills real fast, then slow down to almost nothing as we crept up steep hills, and then we would hold on for dear life as we sped to the bottom of another.

We were at Forest Lake in a few minutes with Gramps at the wheel.

The strawberry festival wasn't fantasyland, such as in my dream, but it came close—tables filled with pink strawberry cakes, strawberry chiffon pies, strawberry shortcakes, and dainty pink strawberry cupcakes. In the corner of the church hall were large containers of homemade strawberry ice cream, vanilla and chocolate. There were strawberry and nut toppings to top the servings of ice cream. Regular and pink lemonade was sold at counters. A man took the change and put it in a cigar box or took change out of another cigar box when he needed to make change. Everything cost 5 cents a serving. I had 35 cents. Wow! I could buy seven things if I wanted to! Gramps bought me a double-dip cone and Gram gave me a piece of strawberry cake, so I bought some pink lemonade. Then I couldn't eat another thing, right then anyway.

With nostalgia I recall the beautifully dressed ladies and young girls with their full skirts and ruffled petticoats, and the boys dressed in dark suits, white shirts and ties; some had white flannel pants and white shoes. The little girls wore pretty organdy or taffeta dresses and black patent-leather shoes; the little boys were dressed in suits, white shirts and ties. The children say they're more comfortable in jeans and things today; in those days, jeans were OK for play or roughing it, but dressing up for Sundays and special occasions was a must. I miss those days!

The magic of the strawberry festival is being revived. Tiny towns and villages and, yes, even cities, are holding old-fashioned strawberry festivals, with homemade ice cream, shortcake and all the fixin's. What a treat to have a strawberry festival just like in the days of old! ◆

### Hasty Strawberry Shortcake

*Here is my recipe for hasty strawberry shortcake my mother made 75 years ago. She used a fork to beat the egg; she had no eggbeater.*

    1 egg
    1 tablespoon sugar
    1 tablespoon flour
    ¼ teaspoon baking powder
    Dash of salt
    1 teaspoon butter

Beat egg until light. Add sugar, flour, baking powder and salt; mix well.

Mix well. Divide among 6 gem pans. Pour shortcake mixture into pans over butter and bake until light brown. With sweetened strawberries and cream, this makes a quick and easy shortcake. Makes 6 servings.

*—Mrs. Golden L. Pitman*

# Kitchen Garden

### By Helen Colwell Oakley

As I was growing up, I wondered what a kitchen garden was. Were the grown-ups going to plant a garden in the farm kitchen? What was going to be planted in it? It couldn't be a very big one because there wasn't room to spare, not with a houseful of children, Mom and Dad, the hired girl and several hired men. Well, when Mom took a notion to have something, her philosophy was "Where there's a will, there's a way!"

Mom remembered visiting a farm when she was a little girl. The lady was preparing dinner in the farm kitchen. She would excuse herself every few minutes and reappear with fresh, crisp lettuce, an onion or two, and then, a huge, lush, red tomato.

The vegetables were freshly picked, so the guests were puzzled as to how their hostess could run to the garden and reappear with vegetables within a very few seconds. Their curiosity got the better of them, so when the hostess dashed out the back door as she was preparing a salad, they crept to the window to look. Just outside the kitchen window was the most beautiful little vegetable garden one could imagine! There were rows, not more than 6 feet in length, of dew-fresh lettuce, onions, radishes, tomatoes and herbs, all to be had right at the back door of the kitchen.

"Well, I never!" exclaimed the guests. "Why didn't I think of this?" each wondered aloud.

The hostess was deeply flattered as the guests admired and praised her lovely kitchen garden. "I have heard about the early settlers having a kitchen garden close to the kitchen door for convenience's sake, so I tried one a few years ago, and find that it can't be beat!" she exclaimed.

Mom remembered how majestically the lady disappeared and then reappeared with her arms full of fresh vegetables. Mom, too, wanted a kitchen garden. Most farm gardens are a good walk from the house, and when a cook wants something from the garden, there isn't always time to dash to the farm garden. But if there is a delightful little kitchen garden by the back door, what could be more wonderful?

Mom got her tiny kitchen garden. How proudly she watched the progress of the tiny plants. She was in her glory as she, too, could run out the back door and bring in a bunch of crisp lettuce, radishes or tomatoes in the twinkling of an eye.

Today, at the Blueberry Farm in Pennsylvania, in addition to the large farm gardens many steps away, there are two tiny, round gardens I can enjoy to the fullest. One is my flower garden and the other is a kitchen garden, sparkling fresh and productive with tiny rows of green onions, bunches of red radishes and vines of delicious tomatoes. A kitchen garden brings much pleasure! ◆

# Chapter 2

⟡

# To the Kitchen

Making do was a way of life back in the Good Old Days. And there was no place making do was more apparent than in our kitchen. We didn't have a dining room; we ate where Mama cooked, baked, sewed— just about everything she did in her busy life. Just like we made do with one bedroom for a family of five, Mama made do in the kitchen without running water, without a gas stove and without electricity.

Mama was a magician in the kitchen. She could have almost nothing in the house to eat, yet come up with a meal that filled our home with such a delectable aroma that it even could pull us from an exciting game of cowboys and Indians in which we were engaged in the front yard. The wafting of that aroma beckoned us to a simple, but wholesome, meal of beans and salt pork, potato soup or Mama's "goulash" as she called it—a kettle of leftovers turned into just one more dish.

Whatever she came up with was spiced heartily with love. That's the same kind of love I hope you find brought by these stories to the pantry of your memory.

—*Ken Tate*

# Grandma's Kitchen

*By Ellen Gallup Genta*

There's always a zesty tang about Grandma's cooking—the aroma of warm, fresh bread, of toast-brown fried spuds and onions, and her spicy pickles will not be forgotten. But, the best grandmother recipe I ever found was one that belonged to the grandmother of Kenneth Roberts, author of *The Kenneth Roberts Reader.* He said there was such a passion for her ketchup that they couldn't get enough of it. She allowed her youngsters and guests to have it on beans, fish cakes and hash, but when they asked for it on a slice of bread, she denied them.

"Then," said Roberts, "we had to go down in the cellar and steal it. I became almost a ketchup drunkard, because of my yearning for it. I begged the recipe from her, and since then have made many a batch of her ketchup."

## Grandma's Ketchup

With a large spoon, rub cooked tomatoes through a sieve to remove seeds and heavy pulp, until you have 1 gallon of liquid in a kettle. One peck of tomatoes, cooked and strained, makes 1 gallon. (A simple method is to use 12 cans of concentrated tomato juice.)

Put the kettle on the stove and bring the juice to a boil. Into a bowl put 1 pint sharp vinegar, and in the vinegar dissolve 6 tablespoons salt, 4 tablespoons allspice, 2 tablespoons mustard, 1 tablespoon powdered cloves, 1 teaspoon black pepper and ¼ teaspoon red pepper.

*In the camaraderie and harmony of the kitchen are the best beginnings of destinies.*

Stir the vinegar and spices into the juice; set kettle over a slow fire and simmer until it thickens. The mixture must be constantly stirred. If made from canned or fresh tomatoes, the mixture must cook 3 or 4 hours.

When removed from the fire, let the mixture stand until cold. Then stir and pour into small-necked bottles. If a ½-inch of olive oil is poured into each bottle, then corked, the ketchup will keep indefinitely in a cool place. Chill before serving.

What might have happened to Grandma's ketchup if early superstitions had prevailed? In early New England, tomatoes were called "love apples," and were shunned as being poisonous. Yet seafaring families had the seed brought from Spain and Cuba by sea captains, and

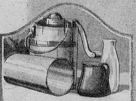

sugar. On a high shelf sat seldom-used and dangerous medicines, and every fall a row of Hubbard squash was settled there. Seems Mom thought a warm, dry place kept them best. Shelves for all the dishes, with wedges to stand the plates against, lined one wall. The bread box, a tight-lidded, square, wooden contraption, always held homemade bread. A three-cornered row of shelves held condiments and spices. There was always a bit of catnip, sassafras and peppermint for teas in case of a stomachache. A large bottle of olive oil, administered with a half-teaspoon of sugar, cured almost any other ill.

Before I went out to herd the cows in the alfalfa pasture, I was allowed a slice of bread, brushed with thick cream skimmed from the milk pan, then sprinkled with sugar. If Mom wasn't looking, there was a good chance to stick one's finger into a settled pan of milk, the cream having risen to the top, and thus making rings with each finger-licking feat.

Under the shelf, two crocks of gray pottery with Dutch blue designs held sweet and dill pickles. For a lid, clean white cobble rocks held plates in just the right place, under the vinegar. It was real simple to lift the plate and fish out a mouth-watering pickle. A soft flour sack, when tucked around them in a bowl, kept raisin-filled cookies or doughnuts fresh and spicy.

The kitchen table was covered by a flowered oilcloth cover, slick and cold to the arms, but mighty easy to clean. Above the table hung a gas lamp, its white mantles ready to shed light over our food. The day when I opened the valve too much, letting gas leak out, and then lit the lamp was almost my Waterloo. I set the tablecloth on fire. Then I threw a bucket of water on the flame, which only spread the flame rapidly over the table. When Mom came from town, she just hugged and hugged my sis and me, and gave us a lecture on how *not* to light gas lamps.

There is much more than a ketchup recipe to remember about Mom's or Grandma's kitchen. Napoleon said, "The future destiny of a child is always the work of the mother," and in the camaraderie and harmony of the kitchen are the best beginnings of destinies, the best flavorings of love, and the best spicing of life. ◆

the wives planted them. Good cooks experimented and came up with sauces of many kinds, and used them as a vegetable rather than a fruit as the tomato is now classed. The sauces, in spite of the aversion to tomatoes, became indispensable with hash, fish and baked beans.

Memories of my mother's kitchen were brewed up by the ketchup recipe. The big, black stove was a beauty. It was my daily chore to fill the reservoir for heating water; I carried water in a bucket from the prime-handled pump way out in the back yard. The stove was trimmed with shiny nickel on the top warming ovens and on the big one at the bottom.

The warming lids, pulled down, made the best book rest one could find, in case you wanted to read while doing the dishes—the dishes being washed in a granite dishpan pushed to the back stove lids. This location was just hot enough to keep the water hand warm. If I heard my mom coming, I could always flip the warming lid shut to hide my folly.

Near the stove was a pantry. Beneath the bread shelf was a barrel of flour and one of

# When Mama Baked a Sample

*By Christie Clay*

The only thing better than licking the bowl when Mama made a cake was eating the sample. The memory of the taste of those small portions lingers with me still and sets my taste buds on edge, even after 50 years.

Of course, the "sample" went out when dependable ovens and ingredients came in. That's progress, and it's a very good thing. The sample, though, is one of my happy childhood memories and recalling it gives me much pleasure.

The aroma from a baking sample of Mama's applesauce cake or prune cake (my favorites) was so tantalizing that my four sisters and I kept near the kitchen when we should have been out feeding the chickens. We knew Mama would call us when the sample was ready to taste and we wanted to be within hearing distance.

I remember watching Mama mix a cake. She'd find a clean newspaper to sift the flour on, get out the pans, a large bowl, the sifter, the wire egg beater, and a measuring cup and spoons.

Then she'd assemble the ingredients. Out came the brown sugar and pecans from their hiding place in the large, crock churn where she kept them because they were endangered species. Oh, I knew about her hiding place, but I didn't let Mama know that I knew.

Mama's cake recipe was apt to be written in pencil on the inside of a split-open, flattened-out cereal box, and it contained a pertinent notation or two, such as "needs a pinch more baking powder."

After mixing came the all-important sample. Mama carefully tested the oven for proper heat by sticking her hand into it, and then she filled a small pie pan with batter.

*Such a little pan,* I thought, but Mama wouldn't spare a lot of batter for the sample. Time seemed an eternity as we waited for it to bake.

Mama cut the sample into five parts with only a sliver left over for herself to see if the batter was right. Sometimes she'd say, "It needs a bit more flour" or some such diagnosis, in which case she'd remedy the batter. Usually she'd pro-nounce it "good." Then we each devoured our share and heartily wished for more.

However, knowing that it was just a sample of the real thing—the delicious, iced and finished cake to come—helped us each to bear the infinitesimal size of our portions with grateful hearts and good humor. ◆

### Five-Egg Sponge Cake

*This is the first recipe I learned to cook, in 1910, when I was about 9. I learned to bake on a beautiful wood-burning stove!*

5 eggs, separated
Pinch of salt
1 cup sugar
1 teaspoon lemon extract
1 cup sifted flour (sift 5 times before measuring)
Preheat oven to 350 degrees.
Beat egg whites until stiff; add a pinch of salt.
In a separate bowl, beat egg yolks until pale yellow. Stir in sugar and lemon extract.
Now fold the egg-yolk mixture and whites together. Fold flour into the eggs. Bake in a tube pan for 45 minutes.

*—Elizabeth Winsor*

# We Ate the Holes

*By Margaret R. Crownover*

The aroma of spices seeping from the kitchen brought my three hungry brothers and me bounding around our big wooden table.

"Move back a little," our small busy mother commanded hastily. Swiftly she crushed the rolling pin against the mound of dough on the white oilcloth.

"Fry us some holes! Fry us some holes!" we pleaded. Our stomachs growled and our eyes bulged. The evidence was all around us. It was doughnut-making day!

"Let me finish the doughnuts first. You know the customers are waiting."

Mother had unexpectedly found a way to supplement our meager income in the summer of 1931 when a neighbor asked, "Mrs. Schneider, will you sell me a dozen of your doughnuts? They smell so good!"

Mother's fame spread quickly, and soon she was selling 30 dozen doughnuts per week at 10 cents a dozen.

We children were delighted. The smells and the excitement of the day were exceeded only by the fact that when you make 30 dozen doughnuts, the cutter also makes 30 dozen doughnut holes. The customers got the doughnuts; the family ate the holes.

Doughnut day started early. By the time the aroma of hot nutmeg came swirling up the stairs to arouse us from our sleep, Mother would have one batch of doughnuts made. We would come downstairs to find golden-brown doughnuts cooling on cut open brown-paper sacks. "Takes up some of the grease," Mother explained.

*In the evening, more children than usual would gather on our front lawn. There was always a treat awaiting us before bedtime.*

Now she was rolling out a second batch while lard bubbled in the big, black, cast-iron kettle on the stove. We begged to help.

"Can I stand on a chair and watch?" I asked as she stood ready to drop a round, flat piece of dough into the kettle.

"Just stand out of the way; this is hot."

She pushed back a strand of long black hair which had escaped the hairpin holding the large bun at the nape of her neck.

The doughnuts were dropped carefully into the hot grease. They would descend to the bottom of the kettle, then pop back to the surface. When the golden-brown color began to show around the edges, Mother would turn the doughnuts quickly.

After what seemed like an eternity, the little flat centers, not much

bigger than a quarter, took their turn in the kettle. They danced and darted and swelled and browned until finally they were ready to come out.

In a large cake tin, the powdered sugar awaited them.

"Don't let them cool too much!"

More sugar would cling to the doughnut holes if they were still warm. Quickly we would pop them into our mouths, sugar hanging on our noses and chins. Soon the kitchen would be covered with powdered doughnuts and powdered children.

"Clean up quickly now and deliver these while they are still fresh," Mother ordered.

My two older brothers would deliver to the more distant customers while my younger brother and I would take the people on our block. What a joy to be the conveyor of such goodies! We sniffed at the bag as we rang the doorbell. The people were always glad to see us, and sometimes we would get an extra penny to keep.

When we returned, the kitchen had been already cleaned and was gleaming. I remember thinking that a magic fairy must have dropped in to help Mother get the job done so fast.

She took the cigar box from the high shelf of the cupboard and the dimes clattered as they hit

the other coins. This money was for special things.

In the evening, more children than usual would gather on our front lawn. There was always a treat awaiting us before bedtime. You guessed it—homemade root beer and doughnut holes.

I owe a debt of gratitude to Capt. Gregory, a Dutch sea captain who, according to the *World Book Encyclopedia,* invented the dough-nut hole in 1847. He cut a hole into the center of the round, fried doughnut cakes to make them more digestible.

A bronze plaque marks his birthplace in Camden Township, Maine. His invention added much to my childhood happiness and to my memories—memories of little, luscious-smelling doughnut holes dripping with powdered sugar. ◆

### Doughnuts in Rhyme

*This recipe was in a cookbook put out by the Ladies Aid Society of Pittsburg, Ohio, many years ago.*

*When I was quite young, Mother told me I could make the doughnuts using this recipe. Being young and inexperienced, I accidentally omitted the line "Baking powder, teaspoons two." Needless to say how they turned out. My older brother said they looked like pretzels. The dog got most of them.*

*I have used this recipe many times, but always remembered that certain line.*

> One cup of sugar, one cup of milk;
> Two eggs beaten as fine as silk,
> Salt and nutmeg (lemon'll do);
> Of baking powder, teaspoons two,
> Lightly stir the flour in.
> Roll on pie board not too thin;
> Cut in diamonds, twists and rings;
> Drop with care the doughy things
> Into fat that briskly swells
> Evenly the spongy cells.
> Watch with care the time for turning;
> Fry them brown—just short of burning,
> Roll in sugar; serve when cool,
> Price a quarter for this rule.

*—Mrs. Waldo Snyder*

# The Pinch & Dab Method

*By Julia Rankin*

**M**any things are mysterious to small children. One that puzzled me when I was very young is just as mysterious to me today, and that is how women of the older generation—aunts, cousins, Mama and her friends—made buttermilk biscuits without measuring anything—unless "a pinch of this" and "a dab of that" is considered measuring. Yet they made light biscuits that were so good and hot with butter, jam, molasses or gravy.

From the time I was big enough to see over the top of the kitchen table I would lean on it, chin on folded arms, and watch my mother make buttermilk biscuits. First she got out the big wooden bread bowl and put about 2½ quarts of flour in it. She stirred a little shallow hole in the middle of the flour, then took a pinch of salt from the saltbox hanging behind the wood-burning cookstove, and sprinkled it on the flour around the hole. After this she took a pinch of baking soda and sprinkled it on top of the salt, then stirred both into a small amount of flour around the hole.

*From the time I was big enough to see over the top of the kitchen table, I would watch my mother make biscuits.*

She scooped up a lump of lard and worked it into the mixed flour. Now, she reached for a pitcher of buttermilk and poured a little puddle in the hole in the mixed flour, and began to stir it all together with her fingers. Each time she went 'round and 'round she took in more of the plain flour that was next to the mixed flour, until she had made a big ball of dough, or maybe a little one, depending on how many people were to be fed.

She punched the dough a few times, then pinched off pieces about the size of an egg, flattened them between the palms of her hands, and put them in rows in shallow pans, much like our cookie sheets today, and put them in a hot oven. If corncobs had been saved from the barn, she added half a dozen to the firebox because they made the fire hotter.

As I watched curiously I asked, "What is the soda for?"

"To make the dough rise up so the biscuits will be light and soft," Mama told me.

"Why did you put salt in them?"

"To make the biscuits taste good."

"Why did you put that dab of lard in?"

"So the biscuits won't be tough."

"What is a pinch?"

"It's what I can pick up with my thumb and forefinger."

"But how can a pinch of salt and a pinch of soda and a dab of lard make a big pan of biscuits or a little panful?"

"Why … er … I never thought of that; I just do it. Maybe I use bigger pinches for more biscuits."

"How does the flour without the salt and soda know how to rise up and taste good?"

"I work it in with the mixed flour."

"But how do you know how much not-mixed flour to mix in?"

"Oh, I don't know how I know; I just know. You ask too many questions for a little girl. I guess everybody makes biscuits this way. When you grow up, you'll learn, too."

But I never did. When I was older I tried, but my biscuits were very bad, the family agreed, flat and tough.

"You didn't get the hang of it," Mama said. "Watch me the next time I make biscuits, then you can make them the same way."

I watched and I tried, but I didn't have the magic touch. There seemed to be some mysterious something that the women of Mama's generation had that I didn't.

When I was in high school I asked my cooking teacher—we called her a home economics teacher—to show me how to make good buttermilk biscuits. She gave me a card from her big recipe file. I stared at it; here it was in black and white, translated into plain English: cups of flour, teaspoons of salt and soda, tablespoons of shortening, the approximate amount of buttermilk, also instructions for mixing and baking: "Sift dry ingredients together, work in shortening, add

*I was happy to see their surprised faces when I triumphantly placed on the table a big plate piled high with light, fluffy biscuits.*

buttermilk and stir with a tablespoon until a soft dough is formed. Knead only enough to make smooth, then roll and cut with a biscuit cutter." It even gave the degree of a hot oven and the number of minutes to bake.

Joyfully I tried it for my dubious family who still remembered my previous efforts. I was happy to see their surprised faces when I triumphantly placed on the table a big plate piled high with light, fluffy biscuits. They voted them as good as Mama's, but I thought they were a lot better. At last I had learned to make good buttermilk biscuits.

In fact, they were so good that some years later my new sister-in-law asked me to show her how to make them. I was flattered. I guess she'd had trouble with the pinch-and-dab method of the older generation, too. I showed her my own treasured recipe card. She copied it, and from that day to this, she makes better buttermilk biscuits than I do. ◆

# An Old-Fashioned Thanksgiving

*By Ellen Tosi*

When we hustled out to the car on those cold Thanksgiving mornings with banks of drifted snow all around us, we could see the white house nestled halfway up the mountain in the clearing, the Bolton Homestead. Here is where we spent all our Thanksgivings from the time I can remember until I was grown-up.

Charles Berger

When my father cranked the old car we hoped that it would start without any trouble. Most always it did after a little sputtering and complaining. Then we were off and down the main road over the river, singing that familiar song, *Over the River and Through the Woods.* That river was the Connecticut, but then we were riding not in a sleigh but in our first car, the Chalmers.

Down by Wanamaker Lake, it was only a short ride before we went onto the narrow dirt road made much narrower by the snow. We passed Aunt Mary's house in front of which was the butternut tree. From this tree she gathered and cracked the nuts for her delicious butternut cake for the party, made in the square tin and cut in squares with a half butternut on each square. She would have already arrived at the big white homestead. From there we went into the more heavily wooded section straight up the mountain.

Our excitement increased by leaps and bounds. As we got to the turn just before we left the woods and came out into the clearing, my brothers and I in the backseat were leaning far out of the touring car to see who could see Grandpa's house first. When it barely came into view we all shouted at the same time, "I see Grandpa's house first!" Then we came out into the opening and there it was, sitting on the brow of the hill, its dormer windows staring down the mountainside.

It seemed almost an eternity to wait as we climbed that last five minutes and finally turned into the driveway at the back door. Now our feelings of excitement and anticipation were at their height. We rushed through the shed over the squeaky floor boards and unlatched the back door.

A blast of warm air from the old wood stove brought wonderful smells of turkey and freshly baked rolls as we came in out of the frosty mountain air.

The first sight would be of my grandfather, sitting in a ladder-back chair by the kitchen window, leaning back against the wall, the front legs of the chair off the floor. There he would sit with that cloud of unruly white hair and violet-blue, sparkly eyes, slim and fragile, his voice husky and a little hard to understand as he spoke. Yet, there was strength in that old Yankee face. He never felt very well; probably because he was wounded in the shoulder at Winchester, Va., during the early days of the Civil War. He carried the bullet from that wound for the rest of his life, and he had a lot of trouble with it in later years. But he was a real hero to us. After he recovered from the wound, he had remained in the Army as a guard in Washington until the end of the war, and he had seen Lincoln. That really impressed us.

There was so much to take in all at once. Our first delight was watching Grandmother in her big white apron proudly open the oven door for us to look at the huge, golden-brown, roasted turkey. We could see the chicken pies in the warming oven above the stove with our favorite cracker pudding. The cakes and pies were lined up on the pantry shelves. The pies were made from pumpkins from Grandpa's garden and the apples from his orchard. He stored the pumpkins and apples in the deepest cellar I had ever seen; the cellar walls were lined with huge stones gathered from the mountainside. Mincemeat was made right there

in Grandmother's kitchen and the vegetables were raised on the farm too.

Uncle Phil always had a keg of cider in the cellar. By Thanksgiving, it had just the right tang to it. It was fun to taste, but we could only stand about one swallow and we were puckering and wincing. The pickles were fun, too; the boys loved to taste the sour cucumber and mustard pickles and then make funny faces.

Dinner in the dining room was for the aunts and uncles. Although the dining room was large, it could not accommodate everyone, so the children had their dinner in the kitchen on the long wooden table with an older cousin. From the kitchen we could hear the laughing in the dining room, especially Uncle Hiram's hearty roar. They reminisced about the old days. Then, when we finished our dinner, we would join them as they sat there, their chairs pushed back from the table. We loved to hear their stories. Usually when you think of older folks reminiscing, you think of people telling of bygone days, almost with tears in their eyes as they tell of the struggles there on the farm. Not these uncles! They always recounted the funny things that happened. They hauled their stories right out of the logging days at Mount Pisgah, or drew them from the days of horses and oxen pulling at the country fairs.

It would be toward 5 o'clock, milking time, and many degrees colder when we left the mountain. We pulled the black bearskin robe, a throwback from our sleighing days, right up to our chins in the backseat of that breezy car as we sped down the mountain.

After these wonderful days passed and my mother and father became Grandmother and Grandfather, Thanksgiving Day for their grandchildren was at their farm by the river. It really was not much different, although Mother never had a dinner party without a centerpiece. For Thanksgiving, she made the prim little Pilgrim ladies wearing black capes over gray dresses with square white collars. The men in long heavy coats and wide black hats led the

solemn procession on their way to church. A gay little plastic turkey from the five-and-ten would be strutting grandly to the center of the stage. When the grandchildren arrived, one of the first things they did was make a wild dash for the dining room to see what Grandma had dreamed up for Thanksgiving.

They arrived by car—but in sleeker models—until the yard was crowded. As Mother and I heard each car drive into the yard, we hurried to the window to see two or three youngsters rushing to the kitchen door, just as we had years ago. There would be a rosy-faced little girl with Shirley Temple curls, running up the path to the back door with a Thanksgiving picture she had made for her grandmother.

Once they were in the kitchen, Mother would also proudly open the oven door to show off her immense browned turkey which my father had raised. A small boy, his feet wide apart, hands in pockets and eyes wide, would ask, "Boy, how big is he?"

After the last car had left we would sit in the living room by the windows. There from our home in the valley, we could see the old white homestead, a Currier & Ives miniature halfway up the mountain. And although we had had a

wonderful day, to us those Thanksgivings we'd enjoyed at the old homestead as children were the best ones of all. ◆

### Thanksgiving Fruitcake

*I make a loaf of this every fall. It keeps well for a year. I keep a plateful, sliced, down in the cellar to keep moist for the table if anyone comes to tea.*

1 cup butter
1 cup brown sugar
1 cup molasses
4 eggs
Nutmeg
½ pound currants
½ pound raisins
¼ pound citron
1 teaspoon cassia (bought in drugstore)
1 teaspoon ground allspice
1 teaspoon ground cloves
1 teaspoon baking soda
4 cups flour
Cream butter and brown sugar. Add remaining ingredients. Mix well. Bake at 325 degrees.

*—Ethel Irene Rundle*

# Sam Morse's Biscuits

*By Donald Kraack*

**M**any years ago, I was "choreing" and minding the house on the old Jacobsen Ranch for my uncles, Ed and Frank Miles while they spent a couple of weeks visiting their families in St. George, Utah.

Ed, cowboy turned rancher, had joined with his brother Frank to acquire a pretty nice spread. The ranch, situated between the small communities of Pine Valley and Central, was isolated from any nearby habitation, and since it contained a turkey flock as well as livestock, someone had to be there constantly.

It was the shank of a warmish but brisk afternoon in early October. Premature ground frost had browned the weeds and grasses in the little valley and blotches of reds and yellows pocked the hills at higher elevations where dense stands of oak and quaking aspen grew. I was standing idly in the half-open doorway of the granary, watching the darkened patterns and leaf shadows shimmering and dancing on the sunny side of the rustic ranch house, as a gentle breeze playfully wafted the mountain mahogany and box elder branches back and forth. I was also mulling over just what to fix for my next meal.

*He was powdery with trail dust, and a growth of several days' beard stubble appeared to almost smother a tanned, leathery face.*

Finally, my gaze focused on the distant, rutted, dusty road extending like a flowing ribbon from the crest of the mountain pass to the valley floor below.

My eyes squinted, pulling my face into a tight grimace as I attempted to visually probe through the wispy autumn haze at an enlarging puff of dust. As it drew nearer, I walked out to the fence gate and soon was able to discern that it was a horse herd driven by a lone rider.

Now, it was a rare occasion indeed to have company at the ranch, either visiting or just passing by. In almost two weeks' time, I had talked to only one man—an Indian on his way to the low country—so this particular visitor commanded my immediate attention.

As he neared the gate where I was standing, he spurred his horse to gallop toward me, and I could see it was the old horse wrangler, Sam Morse. Although he didn't know me, I knew him by reputation and sight.

He slowed his mount to a walk, then stopped, crawled off his horse, and after the usual salutations, tipped his battered Stetson back on his head and said, "I'm trailin' this bunch of horses from the Pine Valley high country down to St. George, and I'd shore like to pasture 'em for a coupla hours or so." He continued, "I'll make it right with the Miles boys, and if you'll invite me to eat, I'll bake you a batch of baking-powder biscuits like you've never et before."

He was powdery with trail dust, and a growth of several days' beard stubble appeared to almost smother a tanned, leathery face. His smallish, beady eyes squinted in cooperation with a copious mouth that hinted a semi-smile. His thinning hair, once-blond was long and graying, and hung down the nape of his neck into a faded blue flannel shirt, opened at the throat to reveal a sun-burned "V" on his chest.

A Durham tag dangled from a pocket, and well-worn chaps covered his frayed, faded, sweaty Levis. His hands were grizzled and rough; it was plain to see he had handled many a bronc in his day, as evidenced by scars, more recent scabbed-over rope burns, and several crooked fingers. Mexican-roweled spurs encased a pair of runover, sharp-toed boots. His general appearance was not unlike that of a Williams Cartoon Character.

But he seemed a decent sort, and as presentable as a man in that capacity could be, so I said, "That's jake with me; I can see

nothing wrong with a deal like that."

I pointed down the road to a wire gate with a pole and chain latch and said, "Open that gate down there and turn 'em in." He made a short loop with his lariat and, slapping it against his chaps, had soon hazed, his herd of 20 or so "broomtails" into the enclosure.

When he returned, we got better acquainted, rolled us a cigarette and "chinned" a bit. "Sam," I said, "you'd better jerk your saddle, water your horse and throw him a forkful of hay. If you're heading for the Dixie country, you've got a far piece to go yet."

After a "thank ya," he dropped his smoke and ground it out with the heel of his boot. "I'll be to the house straightaway. You can show me the biscuit makin's and I'll git busy," he said. He paused, then continued, "I could shore stand some grub."

At the house he tossed his hat onto a wooden peg in the wall, unbuckled his spurs and chaps, and hung them next to his Stetson.

"Make yourself at home," I said. "There's the water basin and pump; I imagine you'll want to wash up a bit."

He had his sleeves rolled up before I had stopped talking.

I threw some kindling into the old Charter Oak, lit it and proceeded to gather the ingredients for Sam's baking-powder biscuits. I started setting the table and sliced some beef for frying. Then I figured I could help Sam by buttering a couple of pie tins and immediately got them from the utensil bin.

Sam spotted the tins and almost hollered. "No, not those! They're no bigger'n bridal rosettes. I need a bread dripper, the biggest one you've got."

I hauled out a dripper that would easily accommodate eight loaves of bread and asked, "Is this big enough?"

"Now that's more like it," Sam replied. " I hate skimpy portions." Then he dove back into the business at hand.

I could see that Sam knew what he was doing. Many years on the range had taught him well. He was as deft in his biscuit-making as any French chef.

My eyes bugged out plenty when I saw him lay the dough in the pan. I swear his biscuits were each as large as a cow clap, and just six of them covered the entire bottom of the dripper. He supervised the oven temperature by insisting he regulate the wood consumption. This part of the meal was his "show," and I gave him full rein. I fried some steak and potatoes and made a pot of coffee. I put a pail of new honey and plenty of fresh-churned butter on the table, then I sat back to await Sam's biscuits.

The biscuits were not too long in coming, and when finally he opened the oven door to draw them out, I gazed upon the most beautiful baking-powder biscuits I had ever seen. This man was an epicurean of the first degree. They were gigantic, a golden tan, and as fluffy and delicate as a summer cloud. A smile played across Sam's whiskered face, and I realized his effort must have been a huge success; pride was showing through.

I served the steak and potatoes, poured the coffee, and we sat down to the meal; I believe few potentates ever dined better than we did that evening. As the saying goes, the hot biscuits "melted in my mouth," and as Sam had promised, they were definitely "nothing like I'd never et before"—or since.

After the meal, we sat, finishing our coffee, smoking and talking. I finally said, "Sam, you and your horse can stay the night if you'll bake me another pan of biscuits before you leave in the morning. It's pretty late in the day to be riding out now, anyway."

Sam agreed. "I'll do just that if you'll fry some more of that steak for breakfast."

I had heard that Sam could trace direct kinship back to Samuel Finley Breese Morse, the artist and inventor of the telegraph. Be that as it may, Sam was just as famous in another line—his biscuits. And that was enough of an accomplishment for me.

We parted company early the next morning, but not before Sam kept his word and made another batch of biscuits. I never saw the old wrangler again, and I don't know if he ever settled with Ed or Frank for using their pasture. But as far as I was concerned, I was well paid, and I believe the Miles brothers would have been, too, if they had ever had the pleasure of eating old Sam Morse's biscuits. ◆

## Baking-Powder Biscuits

2 cups flour
4 teaspoons baking powder
½ teaspoon salt
2 tablespoons shortening (3–4 tablespoons, if a shorter biscuit is desired)
Approximately ¾ cup milk, or mixture of half milk, half-water

Measure sifted flour, baking powder and salt into sifter. Sift into mixing bowl.

Using steel fork, mix shortening lightly and thoroughly with sifted dry ingredients. Add milk slowly, using just enough to make soft dough. Mix lightly with fork. Toss dough onto lightly floured board.

Pat dough out lightly with hands to about ½-inch thick. Cut out with biscuit cutter which has been dipped in flour. Place on greased pan, far apart if a crusty biscuit is desired, close together if you prefer a thicker, softer biscuit. Bake at 475 degrees about 12 minutes. Makes 14 biscuits.

# The Taffy Pull?

*By Jan Wehrlie*

**R**eflecting on fond memories of the past, I am reminded of the fun and excitement of a taffy pull. Just the thought of the taste of that hand-pulled taffy makes my mouth water! The recipe was given to me by my grandmother who got it from her grandmother, so it has been in the family for a long time.

It all started when a friend and I were visiting Grandma and were listening contentedly as she was spinning yarns of the "good old days" (as she remembered them). During the course of her tale, she mentioned a taffy pull.

"Do you know how to make taffy, Gram?" I asked.

"Why yes, I think I can still remember the recipe. Let's try it!"

To our delight, Grandma found the "makings" for vinegar taffy and we decided to attempt our first taffy pull. It was a brisk winter evening, and Grandma said the weather was perfect. She put the ingredients in a pot and set it to boiling. Then she said all we had to do was dip a spoon into the liquid now and then until a drop spun a 12-inch thread.

*Just the thought of the taste of that hand-pulled taffy makes my mouth water.*

That was simple enough, but it seemed to take an eternity. We dipped the spoon into the mixture, lifted it high above the pan, and let it drizzle back in, searching in vain for a thread. For quite some time, all we saw was a little ½-inch thread that turned into a drop. We had both taken turns holding the spoon and were slowly becoming discouraged.

Then the miracle happened. A long thread as fine as a spider web spun down from the spoon and touched the bubbling liquid.

Grandma had us each butter a tin plate and she poured a portion of the thick golden liquid into it. We went out to the porch and started pushing the edges of the taffy toward the center of the plate with a fork, as it hardened. It would ooze out to the sides again and we'd repeat the process until the taffy stayed in a ball.

Grandma said it was time to take it up and pull it. We didn't want to end up with a hardened glob in the middle of the plate, but we couldn't take it up too soon, either, and after a few burned hands, we learned our lesson.

We had to butter our hands so the taffy wouldn't stick to them. To Grandma's horror, two pairs of hands plunged into the neat little cake of soft butter until it looked like Swiss cheese. After a good scolding, we began to pull the taffy. Pull out … put ends together … take middle … pull out, etc. We watched Grandma closely as she deftly pulled her taffy. It looked so easy, but eventually Grandma had to rescue our pathetic yellow strands of taffy with two huge knots at the ends and a thin thread in the middle. Apparently the trick was in the fingertips, but we had to learn that by experience.

The main idea, Grandma explained, was to pull it quickly without twisting the strands, to get air into the taffy. This would make it light and porous. Grandma's taffy glistened like a strand of pearls, its iridescence breathtaking.

However, ours was a different story. Using too much butter on our hands caused our taffy to be a brownish-yellow. We had a tendency to twist the strands and that forced the air bubbles out, so by the time it hardened, it was still thin and sticky.

After Grandma had done all she could to salvage our taffy and we had had a hearty laugh at the sight of it, the strands were pulled out again, this time as far as we could pull them, pulling in doubles, and were laid out on waxed paper and marked with a knife in 1-inch intervals for cutting. Grandma's was so porous and thick and brittle you could snap the pieces off after they were marked, but it was necessary to use scissors on ours!

When the taffy was hard, we wrapped each piece in a small square of waxed paper and twisted the ends. We put our taffy in the refrigerator and hoarded it as long as our appetites would allow. Anyone offered a piece of our taffy was extremely fortunate. It was absolutely too delicious to share.

After our first endeavor, there were frequent taffy pulls, usually occurring when we were entertaining a friend at Grandma's who had never pulled taffy. Naturally, we grandkids became quite adept at it and the guest's taffy was always a hilarious disaster. Once we even dared to try food coloring, hoping for pale pastels, but we arrived at some pretty unappetizing colors.

All in all, I think the old taffy pull ought to be revived for the benefit of all ages. My Great-Great-Grandma Murray's recipe follows, so there's no longer a reason not to try it. Let's help save this dying art. Good luck, and don't be too discouraged if the first batch isn't perfect. It may not look perfect, but the taste is superb! ◆

### Great-Great-Grandma's Vinegar Taffy

For each one pulling:
1 cup cane sugar
1–2 tablespoons vinegar
Enough water to moisten
Pinch of salt
¼ teaspoon cream of tartar
Combine all ingredients in a heavy saucepan and bring to a boil. Do not stir it after it starts to boil; and if crystals form on side of pan, wipe them off with a damp cloth wrapped around a fork. Let mixture boil to the brittle-ball stage or until it spins a 12-inch thread. Do not stir. Pour into greased pan to cool until you can start pulling it.

# The Two "Cookies"

*By Hulda Fletten*
*As told to Tamara Ferrell*

The little alarm clock was ringing as I lay snuggled under the warm quilt in the cook car. It was still too dark to see the numbers on the clock face, but I knew it must already be 3:30 a.m. and time to get up.

"Marie, are you awake?" I whispered sleepily to my bunkmate.

"Yes, Hulda. I'm getting up," Marie answered as we started dressing in our long cotton dresses.

North Dakota's early morning hours in late summer where chilly. The cast-iron stove gave off little warmth from yesterday's banked coals. Marie and I finished dressing by the light of the kerosene lamp. We put on high-heeled, high-topped, black buttoned shoes over white stockings, and coiled our long braids around the crowns of our heads.

Looking into the little mirror on the wall, we carefully fluffed out our hair on the sides and above our foreheads. It was 1907. Being 16 and 17 years old, Marie and I were careful to follow the latest fashions as closely as possible in our farming community.

"You're my two 'cookies,'" Mr. Nelson would say to his daughter Marie and to me. We were the cook-car cooks, making five meals a day for the 30 men who were threshing grain in the end of summer.

As the grain ripened for harvest in late August, Mr. Nelson rented out his steam threshing machine to the farmers around the town of Bisbee. Wherever grain needed harvesting, the thresher would come. First harvested was the barley, then oats and wheat. Finally in October, the flax would be threshed, separated from the chaff and taken in wagons to be sold. Men from Minnesota came to work in the fields, and men must eat. So, wherever Mr. Nelson's threshing machine went, his cook car with the two "cookies" followed.

The stars were fading and the sunrise was lighting the golden fields as Marie set basins of hot water, soap and towels outside the cook car. Inside, I was busy cooking breakfast. The men worked hard and Mr. Nelson wanted good meals ready with plenty of food. I loved to bake and make delicious food for people who enjoyed eating. The men finished washing outside and climbed up the steps into the cook car.

There was a table nailed to each side of the little room and the men sat on stools facing the windows. The two tables were set with silverware, white china plates and cups on colorful oilcloth. Marie served and cleared as I cooked. I stirred oatmeal and flipped pancakes, fried sausage, bacon and eggs, and toasted bread on a grill while boiling coffee. I filled dishes of jams and jellies, pitchers of milk, and pots of coffee. Some mornings, I made waffles sprinkled with white sugar in a cast-iron waffle maker laid on the stovetop. In the cozy white cook car filled with the warm and steamy fragrance of good cooking, the men ate until they were full.

As soon as the men had finished eating, Marie started to wash the dishes and scrub the pots and pans with fine screened sand. Meanwhile, I began to make doughnuts and sandwiches for the men's lunch break at 9 a.m. The first batch of bread had to be placed in the oven, too. Thirty loaves of white-flour and dark molasses-raisin bread had to be baked each day to satisfy the harvesters' appetites.

Lunch was brought to the men where they were working in the fields. Marie and I loaded baskets with egg salad or cheese sandwiches, doughnuts or waffles. Tin cups were used to drink the hot coffee which we brought in 30-cup pots. The threshing machine tooted like a train whistle to signal lunch and the men came and again ate their fill.

Dinner, the largest meal, was served at noon. There was always a roast with gravy, potatoes and vegetables. For dessert I made pies: sweet raisin, custard, and fluffy cream pies with whipped cream on top.

We "cookies" earned our wages well, working seven days a week, rain or shine, during the threshing season. My wages were $3 a day for planning and cooking the meals. Marie didn't enjoy cooking or baking as much as I did so her father paid her $2 a day to wash the dishes and towels, and scrub clean the white wooden floor of the cook car.

If the weather was rainy, the men went into town for the day but returned for meals. Most days, the sun shone brightly and the temperature climbed higher and higher, into the 80s and 90s. We opened the screened windows and door and let a little air in. Outside the hum of the separator droned endlessly and the flies and mosquitoes settled on the screen, attracted by the good smells inside.

After a field break at 3 p.m. for a second lunch, supper had to be prepared. The last meal of the day was served at about 7 o'clock. Soup started the meal. The men especially liked vegetable soup, so I made it most often. A meat dish was the next course. This might be a stew with chunks of beef, beans, carrots, rutabagas and potatoes in a rich gravy. Cabbage slaw was a popular salad. If I fixed a pudding for dessert, there were also fried doughnuts and a side dish of applesauce to go with it.

The threshing machine and separator were quiet now. The evening's dusky coolness settled over the prairie. We lit the kerosene lamp once more to welcome the last men coming in for a late supper. The day's work was hard, but satisfying. As Marie and I brought in our bedding again, and set the alarm clock for another day, it was good to know we had done our job well as "cookies" for the harvestors. ◆

### Favorite Slaw

*This is my mother's favorite slaw recipe to serve to company. I have used it for 52 years and Mother used it before the turn of the century.*

⅓ cup water
⅓ cup sugar
⅓ cup vinegar
Scant ⅛ teaspoon ground black pepper
2½ cups finely shredded cabbage, salted
Boil together the first 4 ingredients for 5 minutes. Pour over cabbage; let stand for about 30 minutes. Cover, weighting cabbage down with a saucer to hold it under the mixture.

—*Mrs. W.R. Worfe*

# Helpers, Not Meddlers

*By Harry S. Goodwin*

On baking days, I hung around the kitchen, underfoot, messing into this and that, wanting to help Grandmother.

"Shoo! Out of my way!" she'd say. Then she'd add, "Interfering hands are not helping hands."

I knew Grandmother was irked by my interference, so I'd scatter out the kitchen door as quick as my little legs would take me.

Now Grandmother was ready to cook. All her food was not baked in the brick oven. Non-interfering helpers were always standing by, each waiting to do its particular chore. Among these helpers were the open fire, ashes and coals of the fireplace, gridiron, bake kettle, Dutch oven, and small wooden planks or slabs of maple or oak.

In the ashes and coals, she roasted chestnuts and potatoes. On the gridiron set over hot coals, she broiled bear, venison and other meats, like homemade sausage. On the gridiron she also brewed her teas of dried mint, blueberry, strawberry or raspberry leaves. She also made coffee substitutes—dried, ground dandelion roots, acorns, crusts of roasted (not burned) rye or Indian-meal bread, or cocoa shells. All these were heated on the gridiron.

To make acorn coffee, she boiled oak acorns in lye for a long time to remove the bitter tannic acid. After a few washings to take away the lye taste, she dried the acorns and roasted them in the hot ashes. The ashes brushed off easily when the acorns were cool. When ground up, the acorns made a good cup of coffee. So did dried, ground dandelion roots.

We could hardly wait for Sunday morning when cups of cocoa-shell drink waited beside our plates. Grandmother made this delicious hot drink by soaking cocoa shells overnight. The next morning, she boiled them in the same water. We stirred in honey and heavy cream, then gulped and gulped the drink until Grandmother said, "Enough! You've drained the pot!"

The bake kettle was a round, iron, pan-shaped kettle with an unturned flange around the edge of the cover. This held hot coals so the bread within would bake on top as well as on the bottom. Grandmother set the bake kettle over hot coals on the hearth. Sometimes she hung it down from a pothook on the crane over the flames.

She made wheatcakes, mixing the batter in a round iron basin which she set in the bake kettle. In 1 teacup of molasses, she dissolved a dab (1 teaspoonful) of saleratus. She mixed this with 1 cup buttermilk. Into this liquid she stirred enough ground whole wheat to make a thin batter. "Always use an iron dish," her "receipt" read.

This basin she put into the bake kettle and then set it over hot coals. With hot coals on top and coals beneath, the wheat cakes cooked through and through. Slices spread with hunks of sweet cream butter made a delightful bread for breakfast.

The bake kettle gave us many tasty meals. One dish that my bulging eyes looked for was what Grandmother called "Mustgodowns." Cousin Sarah gave her this "receipt" which used crusts of rye and Indian-meal bread boiled in water until it looked like hominy grits. Barbados or blackstrap molasses sweetened it. Swimming in slathers of thick cream, one bowl of this was as much sweetness as our ravenous stomachs could devour at one time.

The Dutch oven was a tin cylindrical oven, with one side open toward the fire. Through the middle ran an iron rod or spit. Grandmother pushed this spit through a large ham, leg of lamb, fowl or other meat, and placed it in the notches of the oven. She turned the spit frequently so the meat would be thoroughly cooked on all sides.

Many times Grandmother used this spit to roast a succulent goose, stuffed with her choice, spicy dressing which she used only for goose.

For the goose stuffing, she mixed the ingredients in this order: 2 teacups or more of soft bread crumbs, 1 cup cooked dried prunes, 2 apples, chopped fine, a pinch of salt, a dab of cayenne pepper, a handful or more of sage leaves (if desired), crumbled in the palm, and 4 or 5 big dabs of chopped onions. She moistened this mixture with 1 cup of lard or as much as was needed.

Each time she turned the spit, she basted the goose with the drippings that oozed into the bottom of the oven. This made the goose delightfully succulent.

On an oak or maple slab, Grandmother cooked barvel, shad or any large fish. First she buttered the wooden slab. After she cleaned the fish, she stuffed it with any finely chopped left-over meat and seasoned it with tarragon, peppercorns and salt. Then she covered the fish with bread crumbs. She tied the fish to the buttered slab so it would not slide into the ashes, and set the slab in front of the fire. When it was done, she spread it with a butter-and-parsley sauce, and we ate like gluttons.

She also baked oatcakes on slabs. She made these cakes with 2 teacups of unsifted ground oats, a dab of wheat flour, and a pinch of salt, mixed with a little sour milk. She rolled them thin and let them cook slowly in front of the fireplace. We liked these oatcakes, doused or topped with butter and honey, for breakfast. Sometimes we dunked them into our cups of hot cocoa-shell drink.

The crane and pothooks came into use at every meal. On the crane was the iron teakettle, steaming and ready for service. Pothooks, long and short, hung in a row next to the teakettle on the crane. On these were iron gypsy kettles used to cook soups, chowders and boiled puddings. The puddings we liked best were plum duff and Great-Great-Grandmother Livingston's Scotch plum pudding. She cooked these puddings in cloth bags which had been wrung out in hot water. She dropped the bags of pudding into a kettle of water where they cooked for 3 hours.

Others of Grandmother's "receipts" included parking, berque, johnnycakes, plunkets, cake bread, buckwheat cakes, apple brown bread, brown Betty and dried-apple cake.

All Grandmother's "receipts" form a loving procession through my memory, each more tasty than the last. No matter which one she placed on the table, my lips smacked. "Oh, mmmm! Good, Grandmother! Mmmm, good!"

These cakes were standard breakfast fare long ago, used every day by many families, especially in the wintertime. They were guaranteed to stick to the ribs while one did farm chores or any other outdoor work on cold winter mornings. ◆

# Granny's Little Tin Box

*By Edna Young*

My grandmother was getting on in years when I was born. She would have been considered old by most people by the time I became old enough to visit her.

In the beginning, it was the warmth of her kitchen and the yummy molasses sweet cakes that she always kept on hand that lured me to her house. She promised that when I got older, she would teach me how to make them. Granny always told me, "It's best never to make an honest-to-goodness promise unless you intend to try your best to keep it."

One day when I least expected it, she got out her big wooden mixing bowl and the long-handled spoon, and she gave me the recipe.

I thought the little wood-burning stove was fascinating. Sometimes she would let me throw in a stick of wood when she was fixing the fire. I enjoyed helping Granny gather in wood. She had a long wooden box that she kept setting in the corner behind the stove, and every day we filled it to the brim.

*When I got older, Granny promised she would teach me how to make her molasses sweet cakes.*

I remember how Grandmother was always giving me bits of advice as we worked, and some of it I still rely on. Usually, haste does make waste, and if you do something right the first time, you won't have to do it over. "Cleanliness is next to Godliness" and "Honesty is the best policy" were some of Grandmother's favorite sayings.

Granny firmly believed that herb tea, hard work, and a clean life insured a long life. I always brought out two tin cups for our teatime. I would drink any concoction she served, no matter how it tasted. Sassafras we drank purely for the pleasure. Granny always kept dried red sassafras root in the pantry. She scrubbed it clean, then put it in a kettle of water and boiled it. Then she strained and heated the liquid again, added a little sugar or honey and sometimes a bit of cinnamon. She also used the plain liquid from the brewed sassafras for hair rinse.

Granny had transplanted many wild herbs to her back yard, but the peppermint grew down by the springhouse where the water ran out and made a little creek.

The springhouse was the most wonderful place to go in the summertime. The cold water ran out of the mountain through a pipe into the springhouse and out the other side. The water was channeled through long troughs where Granny kept crocks of fresh milk and butter, sometimes melons and crispy greens, and anything that needed to be kept cold.

I wish I could go back again on a midsummer day, to step inside a cool springhouse, to recapture that special, carefree feeling.

It would seem that Grandmother was a jill-of-all-trades because she did so many things. Every year she made a magnificent flower and vegetable garden. She was talented in sewing just about anything—lovely quilts with a million tiny, identical stitches, and the pretty dresses she made for me, her little helper. But most of all, I loved the rag doll because Granny brought her to life as she put her together and gave her a name, Clara Mae. She became real to me and I loved her dearly.

Granny's little tin box was kept in the trunk where she kept all of her most treasured possessions. She knew how much I loved the time we spent looking through the little gold-colored box with the flowery design on top. It held a lifetime of loving memories, the kind that just aren't made anymore—pictures, of course, of ancestors in their strange dress-up clothes as they stood or sat in solemn pose. My favorite was a picture of a very elegant lady, tall and stately and dressed in what must have been high fashion: a dark, straight, floor-length skirt that had a bit of swirl at the bottom, and a long-sleeved white blouse with wide cuffs and lots of tiny lace. She wore an upswept hairdo, and a round, dark hat sat a bit down on the left side of her forehead. She appeared to have a superb figure. As I looked in admiration, Grandmother would say, "This is your Great-Grandmother Vinable." I hoped with all my heart to grow up to be warm and loving like Granny and beautiful like Grandmother Vinable.

The box held other trinkets: a small silver-colored pin, and a ring that Grandfather made for her when they were first married, which was the most meaningful thing to Granny. There was Grandfather's gold watch chain, and the cameo

locket Granny used to put around my neck every time we got into the box.

Much of my growing-up years were spent at Granny's, enjoying the warmth of her kitchen, the coolness of her spring-house, and the exciting tales of the treasures in the little tin box.

Granny left us a few years ago, but not before adding another treasure to the box, a letter with my name on it and smelling of lavender which always reminded me of her.

"Dear, I'm leaving the little tin box to you, hoping that it will richly bless your life, as it has mine, bestowing riches that are unobtainable with money. May it bring you the wealth of a sunshine girl's smile in the winter of your life, and most of all, may those days be filled with the company of someone as special as you have always been to me."

The legacy of the little tin box has, indeed, made my life richer. ◆

### Old-Fashioned Molasses Sweet Cakes (Or Batter for Dried Fruitcake)

½ cup lard or shortening
1½ cups molasses
1 egg
½ cup thick sweet or sour cream
3 cups flour, sifted three times
1 teaspoon baking soda
1 teaspoon baking powder
2 teaspoons ground ginger

Cream lard and molasses. Stir in egg, then add cream and dry ingredients alternately. Mix well for 2 minutes.

Sprinkle cutting board with sifted flour as needed to keep dough from sticking. Roll dough and cut out with cookie cutter—or, bake paper-thin layers for stack.

# Baking Day

*By Grace Schadt*

**T**oday more than ever, we are aware of our forefathers' and "foremothers'" hard work and back-breaking chores.

When we need a loaf of bread, a quick trip to the corner store is all it takes. Not so for Great-Grandmother. Baking was an all-day affair, usually done once a week. Great sacks of flour were lugged from the mill, usually miles away; water was drawn from a well, much farther than a trip across the kitchen to the faucet, and carried to the house in heavy wooden buckets; eggs were gathered from the chicken coops even when the snow was knee-deep on the ground.

*Find out for yourself the pacifying feeling that comes with the kneading of the bread.*

Great-Grandmother got her milk straight from old Bessie, and salt was chipped from a great block and ground in a mortar and pestle. Only after labored churning was there butter for that delicious taste. I assume Great-Grandmother was smart enough to make it so it could be spread lavishly on the finished product. Always in reserve were the sugar or honey needed to make the yeast grow.

Let us not forget the oven, fueled by logs brought in from the old woodpile. In the middle of winter, the heat from the ovens must have been welcomed, but not so in the summer when temperatures were in the 90s.

All the ingredients are in the bowl or large wooden trough made especially for bread baking. All that is to be done is to add the yeast or sourdough starter that has been saved from last baking day. In many cases, as was the case of Betsy Ross, the starter was passed down from mother to daughter as she set up her own household, and was numbered among the family's most valuable possessions. A living link to the past, it made one proud to think that this bread was from the same bread that her grandparents had been raised on—"the staff of life."

After much mixing, it's time to turn the dough onto a floured board or table to be kneaded. It is hard to describe the feeling of relaxed peacefulness as one kneads the dough over and over, pulling and pushing, adding in just enough flour to bring it to the right consistency, knowing your grandmother surely must have felt the same way when she performed this routine but important task.

It is now time to let the dough rise—free from any draft—to double its size, only to be punched down. The latter was probably done by the children. I don't know why, but there is a thrill when one places one's fist into this great bubble of dough and, *Poof!* It deflates like a balloon, not with a loud bang but with a slow escape of air. The results are a motley mound of dough.

Now a piece of this dough is removed to again be used for our next batch of bread. The loaves are shaped and put aside to rise again till double in size. This time, however, the loaves are carefully placed in the oven to bake. As they emerge, a delightful aroma wafts throughout the house and probably over the entire hillside. This week's supply of bread is done. Next week, the entire procedure will be repeated.

If you would like to put yourself in Great-Grandmother's shoes, try the following recipe. No, you won't have to exhaust yourself; the ingredients are readily available at your nearest supermarket. Find out for yourself the feeling that comes with the kneading and, for a few minutes, step back in time and feel a closeness with our "foremothers" who were surely the "staff" of this country. ◆

### Cinnamon Loaf

*Dough:*
½ cup milk
1½ cup sugar
1½ teaspoons salt
¼ cup (½ stick) butter or margarine
½ cup warm water (105–115 degrees)
2 packages dry yeast
2 eggs, beaten
Approximately 4½ cups unsifted flour

*Filling:*
1½ cups sugar
2 teaspoons ground cinnamon
½ teaspoon ground nutmeg
½ cup raisins

*Glaze:*
½ cup confectioners' sugar
1 teaspoon milk
A few drops of vanilla extract or other
   flavoring

*Orange Butter:*
½ teaspoon orange flavoring
½ cup (1 stick) butter, softened
To make dough, scald milk; stir in sugar, salt and butter; cool to lukewarm.

Into warm bowl, measure water; sprinkle in yeast and stir until dissolved. Add milk mixture, beaten eggs and half the flour. Beat until smooth.

Gradually add remaining flour to make a stiff dough. Turn dough out on slightly floured surface and knead until smooth and elastic, about 10 minutes. Place dough in greased bowl and turn once to grease top. Cover; let rise in warm place until doubled in bulk, about 1 hour.

Punch down and shape. Divide dough in half. Roll out each half into a 9 x 12-inch rectangle.

Combine all ingredients for filling. Sprinkle each rectangle with half of the mixture. Roll up like jelly roll and seal edges firmly. Place sealed edges down in greased 9 x 5 x 3-inch loaf pans. With sharp knife, cut 6 gashes about ½-inch deep across the top of each loaf. Cover; let rise in warm place, free from draft, until doubled in bulk, about 1 hour. Bake at 350 degrees for about 40 minutes.

Combine ingredients for glaze. It should be of a thick pouring consistency. Drizzle over tops of cool loaves.

Combine ingredients for orange butter; spread on bread and enjoy.

# A Free Soup Bone

*By Violet Moore*

With a beef shinbone with a good bit of meat left on it and a "soup bunch," Mother was ready for an early-October ritual that would send me hurtling home from school on roller skates, jumping the cracked places in the sidewalk, negotiating the last bit of narrow walk up to our back steps on one foot and slamming my book satchel down on the porch bench.

Homemade vegetable soup! I loved soup, its smell, its glorious taste, and its long, leisurely preparation. Even the assortment of deep bowls—two plain white, one with roses, and three of willowware—was sacred to the soup ritual.

Summer soups such as cream of tomato or corn chowder were good enough in their time, but they faded into insignificance when compared to Mama's grand achievement in the soup line, homemade vegetable.

The soup bone came free gratis, without charge, wrapped in a length of butcher's paper and tied with a piece of string. Mr. Schmidt gravely agreed with her about roasting the bones in the oven at high heat before putting them on in cold water in the graniteware soup pot. The soup pot had been inherited from Grandma, Mama's mama, and with it a piece of sage soup-making advice: "Simmer, simmer, simmer—boiling is for shirts!"

**Other children's mothers' soups, especially those dumped from a can, were not particularly exciting.**

The simmering went on for a whole afternoon, until the strained broth was of a rich amber color, with pools of golden fat on the surface. The bits of meat that still adhered to the bones were cut up and added to the pot.

But the true construction of the soup-to-be did not begin until the next day. The broth had to stand out in the cool of the back porch all night long. In the morning, Mama would use a slotted spoon to carefully lift the brittle, congealed fat from the top of the rich and quivering jelly and place it, with the bones, in the dog dish.

The wood range stoked, Mama would put the granite soup kettle on a back "eye" and begin to add the ingredients—never quite the same—that made her soup so special. First came a quart of home-canned tomatoes. The tomatoes had been canned dead ripe at the end of the season and had the rich "red" flavor that seems to have been bred out of modern tomatoes.

Next came the celery and carrots and a turnip or two, carefully scraped and cubed. The celery was store-bought, but my little brother was dispatched to the garden to pull up a few of the remaining roots that had escaped the general ingathering for the coming winter.

A bay leaf, a piece of red pepper pod, a bud of garlic into which had been stuck two cloves, parsley dried in the oven and stored in a jar, sweet marjoram grown by a Polish neighbor, and, of course, the "soup bunch" were added. The nickel "bunch" would include a parsnip (which we never grew at home), leeks, green onions, a handful of long snap beans, and other oddments from the vegetable bins. Sometimes we even got okra, which Mama included for the flavor and fished out before serving.

Mama would add only one starch to her pot of soup. It was potatoes *or* rice *or* elbow macaroni, never all three. Occasionally it was pearl barley or even rolled oats, added as a "thickener."

Other mothers' soups, particularly those they dumped from a can and diluted with water, were not particularly exciting, but the flavor of Mama's homemade vegetable soup could never be anticipated. If the soup bone did not yield enough meat scraps to suit her, she would make tiny marble-size meatballs, robbing the 2-pound package of meat-loaf mixture she expected to use for supper, and simmer them a few minutes in the soup. Or if she had added rinsed-off baked beans, she would slice up a few wieners to make "pennies" in our soup.

Slices of homemade bread and plenty of butter were all we wanted with this meal. Let other families munch soda crackers; we preferred the firm, fragrant loaves of whole-wheat bread Mama baked every Saturday. One of my uncles had married a Southerner and his wife introduced what she called "egg bread"—corn bread made with buttermilk, soda, eggs and bacon drippings—to our soup-guzzling crowd.

Excuse me now. I just have to go out and see if some kind market man will sell me a soup bone! ◆

*For men coming in from farm work and children coming home from school chilled to the bone, the aroma of this soup and the warmth of it sure were wonderful. Adjust the amounts of the vegetables to suit your taste.*

1 soup bone with scraps of meat on it
1 cabbage
1 turnip
1 onion
1 rutabaga
3 carrots
1 parsnip
Other vegetables as desired—celery, etc.

Boil the soup bones; remove all edible meat from the bones and return meat to stock. Allow the stock to stand and cool so that part of the fat may be removed as desired.

Chop the cleaned, peeled vegetables in a wooden bowl with hand chopper. Place stock and vegetables in large soup kettle. Season to taste; cook until vegetables are done. Serve piping hot with crackers or toast sticks.

Chopping the vegetables retains more than the modern method of grinding, but either way is good.

—*Ina M. Abrahamzon*

### Old-Fashioned Vegetable Soup

*The following recipe is one of my rich memories of pioneer life in Valley County, Neb., where I was born in a sod house. I lived there until I was 14 years of age. I am now nearing 88 years and still retain keen memories of my girlhood days in Nebraska.*

*Nebraska winters were often cold and stormy.*

CHARLES J. BERGER

# *Christmas Joy*

*By Ruth Conwell*

What was Christmas like when your were a little girl, Grandma?" Beth's question brought visions to my mind of Christmas, as it was at my grandmother's house in Davenport, Iowa, more than 50 years ago.

My fat, jolly grandma loved to cook sumptuous, "down home" meals for her large, always-hungry family. Cooking was the most enjoyable, important part of her day, and she eagerly looked forward to the Christmas holidays each year because they offered her the opportunity to show off her culinary talents. She spent the entire week preceding Christmas preparing a variety of delectable goodies.

*Cooking was the most enjoyable, important part of Grandma's day, and she eagerly looked forward to the Christmas holidays each year.*

Grandma was an expert at making her own candies. We had creamy chocolate fudge made with chopped English walnuts. She cut the fudge into squares, and decorated each piece with half a walnut.

Using a hand-held egg beater, she beat the whites of eggs until they stood up in stiff peaks, and gradually folded a clear, hot syrup into them to produce a delicious divinity fudge.

We buttered our hands for pulling the brown taffy mixture that Grandma poured onto a cold marble slab, then pulled the taffy back and forth until it was shiny and pure white. I sometimes had blisters on my hands from doing this.

Grandma removed the pits from dates, replaced them with nutmeats, and rolled them in sugar.

She baked mounds of assorted Christmas cookies, huge hickory-nut cakes, and we always had meringues that she split and filled with the home-canned strawberries she put up in quart jars every summer.

Each Christmas Eve Grandma brought out a heavy iron pan that resembled a skillet, but this pan had deep round holes in it. She scooped lard from a wooden boat-shaped container and deposited a small portion in each well. This she heated, then dropped a batter of flour, eggs, milk, baking powder and raisins into the hot grease.

The batter turned brown and puffed up, and when done on both sides, emerged from the pan looking like golf balls. She then rolled the balls in powdered sugar. These were especially delicious, but we only had them on Christmas Eve. It was a tradition in our family. I can't quite remember what Grandma called them, but I think it was "fritkins."

Grandma always roasted a goose for Christmas Day. I didn't exactly crave it because I thought it was too greasy. She saved the grease from the goose for medicinal purposes. Perhaps the fact that she rubbed it on my reluctant body if I even *looked* like I was going to cough had something to do with my dislike for the goose.

Germany was Grandma's birthplace. She came to America at the age of 14 after serving an apprenticeship with a baker in Stuttgart, Germany. Following German custom, she celebrated Christmas on Christmas Eve.

One of my uncles would set up our tree in a bucket filled with sand, then Grandma, Mom and Aunt Maggie would let me help them decorate it.

We took needles and thread and strung long strands of blue popcorn (Mom dipped the popped corn into blue Easter egg dye) and cranberries. We cut colored paper and pasted it into small loops to form long chains. We draped the tree with these strands, circling them around the branches.

I felt important to be working with the older folks, and smiled smugly while relishing the envious glances of my cousins, Margie, 8, and June, 4, who had to watch from the sidelines. *After all,* I thought, *they're just little kids.*

I pinched the clamps of the candleholders to open them and attached them to the tips of the tree's lower branches. I can still hear Grandma's voice as she cautioned me, "Just on the tips, mind you, so the candles can't touch the tree and set it afire."

Despite her warnings, someone opened the front door one Christmas, and a draft blew the portieres hanging in the archway into a lighted candle and the curtains started to burn.

Our fox terrier, Mike, had committed a "no-no" on the dining room runner only moments before, and Grandma's scrub bucket filled with soapy water was still standing in the doorway. Uncle Dewey doused the portieres with the water and pitched the tree with all its decorations out the front door. We were fortunate, for the portieres were the only casualty.

When Mom was a little girl, Grandma used a flat iron to crack the nuts for Christmas, but I remember her cracking the nuts with a silver nutcracker. She gave each of us silver picks which we used to extract the nutmeats from their shells. I recall that a large, cut-glass punch bowl with cups stood beside the bowls filled with nuts on Grandma's sideboard. Grandma served Tom-and-Jerrys from it on Christmas Eve.

After an early supper, we youngsters were hustled up the back stairway to an upstairs bedroom to await the arrival of Santa Claus. Our hearts would skip a beat at the sound of a commotion in the parlor followed by a series of "Ho, ho, hos!" and Grandma's eagerly awaited summons: "Hurry on down! Come see what Santa's brought you."

Filled to the brim with anticipation, Margie, June and I nearly fell head over heels in our hurried descent.

We gasped at the splendor of the Christmas tree, proudly bestowing a warm, soft glow on the scene. Then our eyes were sidetracked by the three bulging stockings which hung from the mantel. They were filled to capacity with apples, oranges, and assorted hard candies.

We cried one Christmas Eve because my uncles had filled the stockings with coal and kindling wood to tease us.

There was a wind-up train circling the tree. A baby doll with painted blue eyes stared at us from inside a red doll buggy. It belonged to June.

Grandma bounced a small black doll she'd made from one of Grandpa's socks up and down and kept repeating the words "Hump deedle-dum, hump deedle-dum," over and over. Junie looked into the doll's pearl-white button eyes, and decided that was its name. He became her favorite and she took him to bed with her every night.

A book that Santa brought me contained the fairy-tales of Hans Christian Andersen. I treasured it for many years and sat spellbound as I read the exciting stories of *Rumpelstiltskin, The Goose That Laid the Golden Eggs, Jack and the Beanstalk* and many others.

I also received a Flexible Flyer sled. Christmas Day I tried to lick some snow from one of its runners and my tongue froze to it. I never tried that again, because when I pulled my tongue loose, a portion of my skin stayed on the runner.

For Margie, there was a riding toy called an Irish Mail. Margie propped her two feet on the front axle and gripped a center handle which she pumped back and forth to propel the car forward.

I can hardly restrain my laughter as I recall how Margie, June and I giggled at the sight of my full-grown uncles crawling on their hands and knees up the stairs and down again, playing follow the leader. I know now that one of my mischievous uncles added a bit more spirits to Grandma's eggnog. The members of the family living at Grandma's house were a happy-go-lucky crew to whom I owe my many happy memories.

We got to stay up late on Christmas Eve. We listened to records played on the wind-up Victrola that had a horn and sat on a table in one corner of Grandma's parlor.

Grandma selected records of *Stille Nacht (Silent Night) O Tannenbaum (Oh, Christmas Tree)* and my favorite, *Jingle Bells.* We joined together in singing, some of us off key, the memorable songs.

Whenever she heard *Jingle Bells,* Grandma would reminisce and repeat her oft-told tale of Clodie, the horse who wore jingle bells on her bridle and pulled the family sleigh when Grandma was a girl in Gladbrook, Iowa.

When the strains of *Jingle Bells* had faded away, three tired, happy little misses were herded off to their beds to dream of Santa and the wonders of Christmas at Grandma's. ◆

### Old-Fashioned Potato Candy

*This was my grandmother's recipe.*
Boil 1 large potato until done. Mash until there are no lumps. Add vanilla flavoring. Mix as much sifted confectioners' sugar as needed until the mixture can be rolled out ¼-inch thick. Spread dough with smooth peanut butter. Roll like a jelly roll. Chill and slice in thin slices. Store in plastic or metal container.

*—Susan Oren*

### Chocolate Caramels

5 scant cups granulated sugar
1 cup cream or milk
½ pound unsweetened chocolate
3 tablespoons butter
Combine all ingredients in a heavy saucepan and boil together for 20 minutes, stirring meanwhile. Then try in cold water; if it will crack, it is done. If cooked longer, it will be sugary.

*—Ruby M. Smith*

### Eggnog

*My grandmother used this recipe.*
6 whole eggs plus 3 egg whites
½ cup sugar
1 quart rich milk
½ pint brandy
Grated nutmeg
Whip the whites and yolks of 6 eggs into a stiff cream, adding sugar. Pour into milk, adding brandy and a little nutmeg. Stir and thoroughly mix the ingredients. Then add the additional egg whites, well whipped.

*—Susan Norlan*

# Christmas Smiles & Sugar Cookies

*By Lorene Clark*

*I*f holly wreaths and candy canes
And snowflakes on the windowpanes
And sugar cookies trimmed so fine
Make you smile. . .
It's Christmastime!

As another Christmas season returns, it brings with it a craving for sweet sugar cookies cut out in fancy shapes of a Santa Claus, an angel, a reindeer, a bell, a star—cookies like Nora used to make.

Everyone in town knew Nora. As a young farm girl, she had moved to town to work for the Dietrich family, owners of Bremen's one department store and grocery combined which adjoined Hoople's Tavern on the main street. (Hoople's was a popular gathering place and inspired the comic strip featuring Major Hoople, based upon the proprietor of the establishment.)

Now middle-aged, Nora seemed a permanent fixture in the department store where she was not only a clerk but also a trusted friend of the townspeople. Her trademark was her pencil, used for adding customers' purchases, stuck in the thick knot of hair on top of her head.

It was she who helped make arrangements to buy Christmas presents on the installment plan long before the idea of credit cards was conceived. This year of 1934, she had helped me surprise Mother with a lace tablecloth saved out of my meager earnings received from my South Bend *News-Times* paper route.

During the summer months, she let my sister, Marian, and me have the thick Simplicity pattern books from which we cut hundreds of paper dolls and dressed them in costumes for every occasion.

Mother was ill during the winter of 1933. When the Rev. Mr. Vogel, the pastor of St. Paul's Lutheran Church, asked her who she would like to visit her, Mother replied, "The lady who works in Dietrich's. She's always nice to me when I do my shopping." Mother's answer was the beginning of a long and close friendship.

How we enjoyed eating Sunday dinners at Nora's house! Her long dining-room table held a variety of meats and vegetables accompanied by homemade hot rolls called butter horns and three or four desserts— all fattening.

Sometimes we enjoyed waffle- and-sausage suppers together on Friday evenings.

"When is your birthday, Lorene?" Nora inquired one day. As I answered, she jotted my answer down in a small, well-worn birthday book she carried in her purse. After that, I received a card from Nora on Nov. 18, my birthday, for more than 40 years.

Nora's family had come to the United States from Germany. Dad's had come from Switzerland. Often she and Dad exchanged words in German. Before we ate with Nora, she never failed to say, "Art, will you please say grace?" She meant the long German prayer they had learned as children. We young ones squirmed a bit before Dad came to the "Amen." Then, what happy confusion as the plates were filled from the many platters sent around the length of the table! Beverages were poured: coffee or tea for the grown-ups and milk, fresh from the farm, for the children.

"Dora Tyler has a quilt in, Mabel. Do you want to go help her out with it?" Nora asked one afternoon as Mother bought a spool of thread in Dietrich's store. That evening Mother had supper on the table early so she could stop for Nora on her way to Dora Tyler's. The snow creaked under their feet, but they were soon warmed by the welcome of the other ladies already gathered in the big, white house on Plymouth Street.

A group of 10 or 12 women could sit comfortably around the quilt frame, so a

*At Christmastime, Nora was especially busy. Two to four weeks before the holidays, she hurried home from work to bake cookies. Christmas, to me, meant cookies from Nora.*

quilting was a real social event. A lunch was a required ritual of a quilting. "Lunch" is a misnomer as some ladies, not to risk being considered poor hostesses, presented an array of prepared dishes to equal a banquet. A quilting could make or break a housewife, and was not to be taken lightly!

At Christmastime, Nora was especially busy. Two to four weeks before the holidays, she hurried home from work to bake cookies.

Christmas, to me, meant cookies from Nora.

How plainly I see her, even now, in my mind's eye: a plump woman with a shining face coming through our door. Her eyeglasses are steamed from the frosty air and her nose is red from the biting cold of our Midwest winter, for she has walked the five blocks to our house.

We are prepared for her entrance—Dad, Mother, Marian and I—for we hear her stomping the snow off her black rubber snap boots as she crosses the wooden porch. On her face is a warm smile to melt the ice and snow about her.

"Anybody home? Merry Christmas to you folks!" she calls out as she opens the door with her free arm. On her other arm hangs a familiar wicker basket. It has a cover; the two sides fold up and open and close from the middle. It has been carried to numerous church socials, potlucks and family reunions.

Seeing that basket brings cheer to my childhood heart, for I have previously tasted its wares—a dessert pudding made with graham-cracker crumbs (Nora keeps the recipe a secret through the years), moist cakes and tasty pies. Now, at this Yuletide season, I know my favorite will be produced from its depths.

"These cut-out cookies are for you, Lorene," Nora says as she hands me a large oval holiday tin. Her eyes twinkle as she observes my pleasure in her gift.

"My, we have been busy at the store— haven't had a minute to spare, I'll tell you. How's it going, Art?" Nora keeps up a steady conversation as she unpacks her delicacies, and Mother scurries to the kitchen to put a pot of coffee on the stove.

As the grown-ups visit, I survey my treasure. The wonder of the delicate figures amazes me. I memorize the storylike shapes of each before savoring it. The thinner ones melt in my mouth. The thicker ones, Nora says, are good "dunkers," just right for dipping into a cold glass of milk or a steaming-hot cup of coffee.

Nora has brought other cookies. Many are of German origin, as Bremen, Ind., our hometown, was settled by German immigrants, and the customs from the "old country" are handed down from one generation to another. From Nora's box Dad picks out a *springerle*, rolled out with a specially designed rolling pin. Anise cookies are popular with Aunt Anna, Dad's sister, who bakes cookies, also.

### *Do you suppose some day, 30 or 40 years from now, a little girl will remember the lady who brought her cut-out sugar cookies?*

Let the grown-ups feast on the others! The sugar cookies hold me in their magic spell as do the stories in my third-grade reader.

The room rings with the sound of happy voices. The fragrant aroma of coffee and freshly baked cookies fills the air. Sandy, the little rat terrier, snoozes contentedly beside a little girl who soon joins her pet in a sweet and peaceful slumber.

Nora is gone now, but her memory lives in my heart, nurtured by her many kindnesses. My mouth waters for a taste of her sugar cookies, so yesterday I got out my rolling pin, rolled out cookie dough and cut out tiny figures and baked them in the oven. Today I packed them into boxes and delivered them to my neighbors and their children.

Do you suppose some day, 30 or 40 years from now, a little girl will remember the lady who brought her cut-out sugar cookies, just as I remember Nora doing so long ago? I pray it will be so, and I also pray she will find a recipe and mix the dough and roll it out, cut it into delicate shapes, bake them in the oven, pack them prettily and deliver them to her neighbors and their children.

It is important not to break the fragile chain of Christmas. One way to strengthen it is with Christmas smiles and sugar cookies.

I do not have Nora's recipe for sugar cookies as she kept it in her head, but here is the recipe I use. If you try it, your kitchen will smell like Christmas and taste like it, too! ◆

### Sugar Cookies

4½ cups sifted flour
½ teaspoon salt
1 teaspoon baking soda
1½ cups sugar
1 cup softened butter or margarine
1 teaspoon vanilla extract
3 eggs

Into a large bowl, sift together flour, salt and baking soda.

In a separate bowl, cream together sugar and butter; add vanilla and eggs to the creamed mixture.

Now gradually add the flour mixture to the creamed mixture. Mix it well and carefully. If you use your hands, as I do, flour them first so they won't stick to the dough.

Working with a small portion of the dough at a time, roll it out out and cut into shapes with cookie cutters. Bake on cookie sheets in a 350-degree oven for 10 minutes. (Ovens may vary.)

*Note:* Before rolling the dough, you may like to place it in the refrigerator. It helps to roll it out more smoothly.

Cookies may be frosted, if you desire.

### Frosting

1 cup confectioners' sugar
1 egg white
Few grains salt
Vegetable food coloring
Extract for flavoring: vanilla, lemon, etc.

Gradually add confectioners' sugar to unbeaten egg white and salt. Beat until smooth and of a consistency to pour slightly. Divide frosting into two or three small bowls and color in pastel shades with vegetable coloring; flavor as desired.

# My Heritage

*By Josie Patrick*

The countryside is a lovely place in the fall. The woods are aglow with vibrant colors: red, yellow, orange and gold. It's as if all the leaves are decked out for a finale before the curtain is drawn.

Against the crimson sunset is flung an elongated V-shaped flock of geese. Their honking reminds me that winter is near.

I feel a nip in the air and nostalgia sweeps me. I recollect days gone by. I remember the fun of jumping over mounds of freshly raked leaves, the crackle of the leaping flames consuming them, and also the acrid smell of smoke.

**I feel a nip in the air and nostalgia sweeps me.**

I remember the coziness of a kitchen with logs blazing in the fireplace and a kettle hanging from the crane, a wood stove with collard greens in a black iron pot, corn bread in the warming closet, and yams, with syrup oozing from their jackets.

I remember the excitement of hog-killing day, the path to the barn frozen stiff, the coldness of the white rime through my high-top shoes, my breath turning to wisps like smoke.

I remember hams and sides of bacon slung from the smokehouse rafters, a smoldering pit fire, the long salting table and large open box awaiting the cured meat. I remember the trips to the neighbors, carrying freshly wrapped parcels of backbone, ribs and liver, the smiles on those people's faces, and the affection in their voices.

I remember all this with a touch of longing—and a prayer of thankfulness for my country childhood, my rich heritage. ◆

### Grandfather's Old-Fashioned Pork Sausage

10 pounds lean ground pork
4 ounces salt
1 ounce pepper
½ ounce powdered sage
½ tablespoon ginger

When sausage is cool, pack in crocks or pans. Cover thick with lard and with paper (heavy white paper preferred with no printing on the paper). Keep cool in dark place. Each time after taking some out for use, pack the lard on the opening, then close it tightly with paper.

—*Lorena E.S. Jones*

### Brine for Corning

*Butchering in the fall brought some good eating. A good way of preserving was corning. We did it this way:*

2 quarts water
¾ pound salt
¼ pound brown sugar
¼ ounce saltpeter
1 teaspoon ginger
3 bay leaves
2 cloves garlic

Combine water, salt, brown sugar and saltpeter in a granite saucepan and heat to boiling. Let cool; then strain through cheesecloth.

Pour brine over the meat; add ginger, bay leaves and garlic.

This amount of brine is sufficient for a dozen tongues. Calf tongue may be cured in the same way and, if desired, a piece of beef may be corned in the same brine with the tongue.

### Pickled Pig's Feet

*"Pickled pig's feet, too!" You'll smack your lips. Here's how to make them the old-time way.*

Scrape and clean pig's feet thoroughly. Put in kettle and boil for 4–5 hours, until soft, adding salt to taste during boiling. Take out and pack in a crock or stone jar.

Boil vinegar and spices well; pour over pig's feet until covered. Allow them to stand for several days before serving.

### Virginia Spoon Bread

*Folks don't seem to cotton to spoon bread much any more. With the coming of fall and the smell of winter in the air, nothing hits the spot like spoon bread. I made it this way:*

½ cup hominy
1 quart water
2 tablespoons salt
3 eggs, beaten

*I remember the coziness of a kitchen with logs blazing in the fireplace.*

4 tablespoons cornmeal
1½ teaspoons baking powder

Add hominy to water and cook for 25 minutes. Then add salt, eggs, cornmeal and baking powder. Blend, then beat. Pour into a well-greased dish. Bake for 45 minutes. To serve, spoon it from the dish.

—*Algene Carrier*

### Salt-Pork Cake

2 cups boiling water
¾ pound fat salt pork, finely chopped
2½ cups sugar
½ cup molasses
2 teaspoons baking soda
2 cups chopped raisins
6 cups flour
½ teaspoon ground cloves
1 teaspoon ground cinnamon
1 teaspoon ground allspice

Pour boiling water over salt pork; let stand until lukewarm. Blend in remaining ingredients.

Divide mixture among 3 small or 2 large loaf pans. Bake at 350 degrees for about 1 hour 15 minutes.

—*Doris Meunier*

# Chapter 3

## To the Table

When Janice and I started our family decades ago, we agreed that food would not be all that we brought to the table. Served up with the meal would be religion, politics, sports, philosophy—all the courses of life that gives it spice. Our three children learned to sandwich conversation between fried squash and onions, pot roast, potatoes and fresh apple pie.

"Why did God make wasps?" "Where did that baby calf come from?" "Why doesn't Bobby like me?" Those were the kinds of questions passed around the table along with the black-eyed peas. They came to see that Mama and Papa didn't have all the answers, but that we didn't mind talking about whatever they brought to the table.

When I see more and more families taking their meals in front of the television, I fear we are losing an important part of life. Meals when Janice and I were children—and when our children were children—were about more than nutrition. They were also about questions and answers, fears and wonders, doubts and assurances—all brought to the table of life.

—Ken Tate

# Baked Beans & Baths

*By Edwin J. Allard*

Weekends in the mid-'20s were memorable for two very good reasons—baked beans and baths. It is hard to remember a Saturday night when there wasn't a large dish of baked beans, crowned by a generous hunk of salt pork, occupying the place of honor on the supper table. Fresh from the bean pot, their steamy vapors filled the room with mouthwatering aroma. Yellow eyes, red kidneys, Jacob's cattle or pea beans—it made no difference. A dash of vinegar with just the right tartness, a crusty slice of homemade bread or steaming brown bread filled with raisins, made a baked bean supper a feast fit for kings.

Sated, we would let out another notch in our belts and back away from the table to let our supper settle before we took our Saturday-night bath.

Taking a bath in those days was no easy task. Few homes had bathtubs and a shower was a downpour of rain. Privies still stood in backyard isolation at the end of a well-worn path, and plumbing had a long way to go. Because of the preparation involved, it was considered socially adequate to bathe once a week and the weekly ablution came to be a regular event of the weekend. During the week we washed at the kitchen sink or at a wash basin placed on a bench just outside the kitchen door. The sudsy water was said to be good for the flowerbeds.

On Saturday night, the dishes were quickly washed and put away and the kitchen became a beehive of activity. Father stoked the fire with wood that crackled and roared as he adjusted the dampers. Countless trips were made with dippers full of water to fill the stove reservoir and a motley collection of pots and pans. A trail of dribbled water across the kitchen floor marked our progress.

While the water was heating, we spread old newspapers on the floor close to the oven door and Father lugged in the galvanized washtub from the woodshed, placing it carefully on the papers.

In no time at all the teakettle began to hum merrily and

the pots began to send up wisps of steam. Father would herd the rest of the family into the parlor and once the coast was clear, we began dipping the hot water into the tub, tempering it with cold water from the sink.

Quickly, we shucked our clothes, tested the temperature of the water with a reluctant toe and hunkered gingerly down into the tub. Squatting in that ludicrous position, we wrestled with an obstreperous washrag and a slippery bar of soap. Inevitably the soap would slip from our grasp and skid across the floor just out of reach.

Standing in the tub and dripping noisily on the newspapers, we would stretch and bend to retrieve the elusive bar. A careless bend, back to the stove, could bring forth a painful yelp that would bring the whole family running. That, and trying to reach the tender blister with unguents, could be most embarrassing. Ignoring the sly snickers of the family as we sat down cautiously was difficult.

It seemed that the fire always began to die down near the end of our bath, and as we stood to towel off, our skin would cobble with gooseflesh. Barely dry, we slipped into clean long johns and shoved fresh sticks of wood into the firebox, listening happily as the embers snapped and popped and began to blaze again.

We used the dipper again to empty the tub. When it was nearly empty, Father would answer our call and, as he tried not to grin at the sight of me in my knobby-kneed underwear, he would help me lift the tub to the sink to empty it, usually splashing the floor in the process and enriching my vocabulary.

Pots and pans would be refilled, puddles mopped up and fresh, dry papers spread. By the time we were dressed, tendrils of steam would be rising from the stove and the kitchen would be warm and cozy. Scrubbed and shining, we would then go into the parlor as the next bather claimed the privacy of the kitchen. It was a time of delightful contentment. ◆

### Baked Beans

1 pound pink beans
1 pound salt pork
Salt to taste
2 large onions, chopped
1 large can tomatoes, chopped
2 cups sugar
Pepper to taste
Soak beans and pour off the water several times. Then add salt pork and salt and cook until tender. Add onions, tomatoes, sugar, pepper and more salt to taste. Bake in an oven or over a slow fire and let cook for hours; Father says, "The longer the better."

—*Nellie Malone*

# Cupid & The Peach

*By B.C. Heisler*

Nothing about man weathers better than his memory. Nippy mellow as a favorite cheese or sparkling as a vintage wine, memory sustains and comforts him in his declining years, and lets him glimpse himself as hero in some little drama played upon his own small stage long years ago.

I was thinking along that line at the dinner table when my wife remarked that no pie is more delicious than fresh peach.

"Peach pie is best," I agreed.

But I was not thinking of Vella Mae's pie made of picked-green, shipped-to-market peaches. I was remembering Becky's pies made of home-grown, tree-ripened fruit, each juicy serving topped with a golden blob of whipped cream … or, peach season over, that special treat of hers, dried-peach pie!

It was August and the day was off to a blazing start by the time my morning chores were done and a basket was filled with the bushel of peaches Mrs. Dawson had ordered.

"I'm glad you have the peaches ready," Aunt Cammie said. "Jeb's mother called to say that he is on the way here. Jeb's a man who doesn't like to be kept waiting."

As I went back into the yard, I saw Becky, Aunt Cammie's hired girl, carry a bucket of halved peaches up the ladder to the corrugated-iron roof of the buggy shed.

The spirit of mischief that possessed me just then was born, no doubt, of a 9-year-old boy's disappointment over seeing his cowboy idol run a poor second in Becky's affections to a certain prosperous farmer. I watched her go about laying the peaches upon the roof to dry, and when her back was turned I slipped up to the shed and eased the ladder to the ground. Back over the stile, I climbed high among the branches of an elm tree. With the supply of ripe peaches that I kept stashed in a small bucket tied to a limb of the tree, I lolled in ease while I waited for Becky to discover that she was trapped on the hot roof.

Placing peaches in golden rows, she sang *In the Shade of the Old Apple Tree,* a song she'd learned from the phonograph in Aunt Cammie's parlor. However, I missed the happy lilt that had been in the song the night before when she sang it for Henry Hughes, a tall, gray-eyed cowboy who worked for my aunt that summer.

Evening chores done, Henry and Becky had sat together on the side porch just off the bedroom where I was supposed to be sleeping. When Becky finished the song, I heard Henry say, "You ought to be the one singing on the phonograph, Becky. You make that singer on the record sound like a roupy canary."

Henry must have kissed her then, for Becky said, "I might have guessed where your sugar talk was leading."

"What's wrong with sugar talk when two are in love?"

"Nothing," Becky answered. "Only …"

"Only I don't own a fine team and a rubber-tired buggy," Henry cut in. "I don't have a four-room house with a fancy porch on my quarter-section of grass over on Cache Creek. That's it, Becky. That's what stands between you'n me!"

Impatiently I had listened for Becky to break the hurting silence with denial that Jeb Dawson meant anything to her. When she didn't speak, Henry went on, "You know that I love you, Becky. Will you marry me as soon as I get our place fixed up a bit?"

Like a skittish colt, Becky shied away from a

direct answer. "The trouble with you, Henry …"

He didn't wait for her to finish. Becky would have had to have been deaf not to hear the ache in his voice when he said, "Speaking of trouble, reckon I won't trouble you more. I've finished my job here with Mrs. Walker. I'll be striking out for Cache Creek tomorrow. Goodbye, Becky."

From my perch in the elm, I watched Becky take off her starched bonnet and fan herself with it. No longer singing the apple tree song, she sat back on her heels, looking first one direction, then another. All of a sudden, she clapped the bonnet over her honey-colored hair and went back to spreading the peaches. Henry was riding into the barn lot!

At the water tank, he slipped off the bridle so the roan could drink free of the bits. Though Becky was in plain sight there on the roof, if he saw her, he didn't let on, and Becky kept any interest she had in him hidden beneath the pink bonnet. But from the fluttery way she worked, it was easy to tell that something was yeasting in her mind—probably my aunt's pointed remarks that morning after Henry ate his breakfast and rode out to the pasture to make a final check of the cattle.

"Henry's a fine, upstanding young man," Aunt Cammie had said. "A girl could do worse than marry a man like him." Her floured hands resting on the bread board, she went on, "Being orphaned as you were, I can see why you set such store by a home, but don't mistake a house for a home, Becky. A home doesn't come ready-made. It comes with the years, with two who love working and building together."

Maybe Becky was remembering that now, for when the horse had finished drinking and Henry started to ride away, she called after him, "Henry, please wait. I want to see you a minute." She went scrambling down the roof to cry out in dismay when she discovered the ladder upon the ground. "Henry, oh, Henry!"

From the way he turned back at her call, a

*What's wrong with sugar talk when two are in love?*

happily-ever-after ending seemed in sight, but at that moment Jeb Dawson drove into the yard, the bay team sleek and glistening in the sun, the black buggy fine and as respectable looking as Jeb himself, who was dressed in his Sunday-best black-and-white checkered pants and a starched white shirt. A flat straw hat covered his balding spot.

Tying the team to the hitching post, Jeb practically flew over the stile. "Rebecca! You shouldn't be up on the roof in this sun!"

Maybe she was disappointed that Jeb's appearance had stopped Henry from coming at her call, for there was a note of petulance in her voice when she said, "Set the ladder up for me, Jeb. For all some folks care, I could cook alive on this roof."

*Being orphaned as you were, I can see why you set such store by a home, but don't mistake a house for a home. A home doesn't come ready-made. It comes with the years, with two who love working and building together.*

Jeb didn't bother with the ladder. Instead, as full of strut and showoff as Aunt Cammie's Dominique rooster, he stepped directly below where Becky sat and reached with open arms.

"Come on, Peaches," he urged in syrupy tone.

That's when Cupid came upon the scene to let fly the squishiest peach in the bucket!

Unfortunately, I did not freeze into a state of shocked disbelief as did the others, and so was betrayed by movement of my leafy curtain as I tried to make myself small within the arms of the tree.

"So!" Becky cried. "You threw that peach! You moved my ladder!"

Jeb's squawk as he mopped the mess from his face and the way he looked up at me made me think that I had better scat higher in the tree, but Becky ordered me to the ground.

"Jeb's due an apology for your scandalous

behavior," she scolded. Then, in the next breath, she burst out laughing. Her words punctuated with giggles, she said, "I'm sorry, Jeb, but … but it's all so funny!"

Simmering like a pot of peach butter about to boil over, Jeb snatched the ladder from the ground and set it against the shed. "Get down from that roof, Rebecca!" he ordered. "Try acting like a lady for a change!"

That sobered Becky. Looking at Jeb intently as though seeing him for the first time, she asked, "Whose lady, Mr. Dawson?" With the toe of her slipper, she pushed the ladder to the ground.

"Are you crazy?" Jeb demanded.

"Not any more," Becky answered, not looking at Jeb but at Henry, sitting yonder in the saddle with pretended indifference.

Six weeks later there was a charivari and housewarming at Henry's cabin on Cache Creek. Finally, the boisterous clamor over, Henry invited the serenaders inside. He grinned good-naturedly at their teasing remarks as he passed cigars to the men, while Becky, wild-rose pretty in pink gingham, served each guest a juicy wedge of dried-peach pie. Each guest, that is, except one. I had two servings of that pie. Henry saw to that.

———✦———

"Well!" Vella Mae exclaimed with a twinkle in her eye. "The look on your face as you ate that pie tells me that all the extra time I spent in the kitchen this morning is worth the effort."

"Mmm … delicious!" I assured her, and with my napkin wiped from my lips the Jersey cream that had topped my second helping of Becky's dried-peach pie. ◆

### My Grandmother's Recipe for Peach Potpie

To make a delicious peach pot-pie, fill a pudding pan one-third full of peaches, pared, stoned and quartered. I slice each half-peach into 6 pieces. Pour 1 cup boiling water over them and set on stove to cook with ⅔ cup of sugar stirred in them.

When they begin to boil, lay a crust made of

biscuit dough over the top. (When I make my biscuit dough, I add ¼ cup sugar.) Cover closely and bake for 20 minutes, or until biscuits are light golden-brown. Serve with cream or eat plain.

—*Miss Dorothy Lybarger*

### Peach Float

1 pint of milk
2 eggs
3 tablespoons sugar
1 tablespoon flour
Preserved peach halves
Whipped cream

Make a custard of the milk, eggs, sugar and flour. Cook until thick. Pour into glass dish. Put halves of preserved peaches into dish and dot with whipped cream.

—*Mrs. Dorothy Lennon*

### Peach Pickles

*This is a very old recipe, over 100 years old, handed down by my grandmother, Mrs. D.S. Christopher.*

1 pint vinegar
3 pounds sugar
7 pounds peeled cling peaches
Whole cloves

Let vinegar and sugar boil together for a few minutes.

Drop peaches into the syrup. Cook until you can pierce peaches with broom straw. Drop a few whole cloves in each jar.

—*Mrs. Floyd McLaughlin*

# Put the Coffee On

*By Joseph Jankowski*

I grew up in upper New York State. Life in our family was probably that of any large family; there were seven children in ours, four boys and three girls. While we had our share of petty arguments and misunderstandings, we also enjoyed a good measure of funny and most memorable events.

Having been born in 1925, I grew up during the Depression. Of course, at that time I neither knew what a Depression was, nor of the struggle parents faced to keep food on the table and clothing on the children's backs.

Pop was a fireman on the railroad, and fortunately worked quite regularly. Compared to most families, I guess we lived on Easy Street. If we were poor, I didn't know it. Pop always seemed to have a garden and he raised chickens, too. I'm sure that helped to see us through. I do remember that we had chicken almost every Sunday, and that must be why, if I have chicken only once a year, I'm content.

*We stopped along the way and called her, telling her to put the coffee on and not to worry. Frank figured if she had something to do, she might worry less.*

In the winter, the boys in the family would go to the nearby creek and chop ice to make homemade ice cream. Of course, sledding downhill or snowball fights took place along the way. Back home, we took turns cranking the ice-cream maker, and every seventh time, when this job was completed, it was my pleasure to lick the remaining ice cream off the paddle. That seventh turn seemed forever in coming around.

I must have been about 10 years old when my eldest brother, Frank, joined the Navy. That's when it started—our family get-togethers over coffee. Every time Frank came home, he would call Mom as soon as he got to town and ask her to put the coffee on, and that he'd be home in a few minutes.

How happy Mom was when she received Frank's unexpected calls! Soon all available family members would gather at home to sit and talk with him over coffee. It became a very special time and a tradition at our house.

As the years passed, brothers Tom and John also went into the service, Tom into the Navy and John into the Army. That left me as the only boy at home. I looked forward to the times when one of my brothers would call and, following Frank's example, ask Mom to put the coffee on, as they were in town.

It was a pleasant time, especially when Pop was at home, too. He was on the road a lot, running trains.

The boys would relate where they had been and the things they had seen and done. It goes without saying that it was interesting and educational for all of us. Frank traveled to several ports overseas and it was always fascinating to hear him tell of faraway places.

In about 1939, Frank was discharged from the Navy and came home to live. Mary, my eldest sister, was married by now; Josephine and Martha and I were still in school.

Tom and John were missed, but when the family did get together around the kitchen table, there were always stories to tell and experiences to relate.

Once when John was home on leave, Mom couldn't resist telling about the time he came home from a date. As Mom told it, he ran upstairs to his bedroom, and without turning on the lights, undressed and leaped into bed. But to his surprise, he hit the floor; only the bed frame was there! Mom had taken the mattress and springs off the bed earlier that day, and had forgotten to put them back. My gosh, how we all laughed over that—including John!

Our get-togethers over coffee were special, like family reunions. They brought us a lot of laughs, and helped us solve problems. They were perhaps the one event for which each of us made a special effort to get together, to share each other's latest news and views.

Around 1940, Frank was working, John and Tom were still in the service, and Mary now had a couple of children. Jo and Martha were still in school, with me. Mom and Pop were well, and I was working after school peddling papers, trying to make enough money to pay them back for the bicycle they had bought me.

Jo bought a record player and at times she would let me use it. I'd play the latest records, making believe I was on radio, announcing the song and the artist like the deejays I'd heard so often. Who was to know that some 26 years later

I would actually become a radio announcer?

Over the years, Frank had gotten into horseback riding. One Sunday, he took me and a friend with him. We all enjoyed the ride, and were preparing to return home when we heard about the attack on Pearl Harbor, in Hawaii. It was Dec. 7, 1941, a day many will never forget.

Frank realized what it meant. He knew that our brother Tom was probably there; at least his last letter had said he was. We rushed home to be with Mom, knowing she would worry. We stopped along the way and called her, telling her to put the coffee on and not to worry. Frank figured if she had something to do, she might worry less about Tom.

When we reached home, most of the family was already there. Mom had somehow managed to make coffee and call the family together. We listened as Frank tried to ease Mom's fears. "Let's wait and see," he said. "He might not have been there." I don't think the younger members of the family realized the seriousness of the bombing; I know I didn't. But somehow, the beautiful day had turned into a nightmare.

Several weeks passed with no word from Tom. The waiting was hard on everyone, especially Mom and Pop. We tried to comfort them with the words that Mom had always expressed to us before—that no news is good news. We hoped it was true, that Tom was safe.

Finally, one day, Joe, our mailman, pounded on the front door, yelling, "It's here, it's here! A letter from Tom!" Joe knew the situation. He had been on our delivery route for a lot of years. He watched all of us kids grow up. He said he was sorry he didn't notice the letter sooner; he would have called. He was that kind of guy, a real friend.

Tom was OK. He had been at Pearl, but his ship was able to be put out to sea and avoid any serious damage. John was notified of Tom's letter. Once again, the family was able to smile.

Soon after, Frank went into the Army. Our front window now had a banner with three stars on it.

A few weeks later, the phone rang. The usual request that Mom put the coffee on was

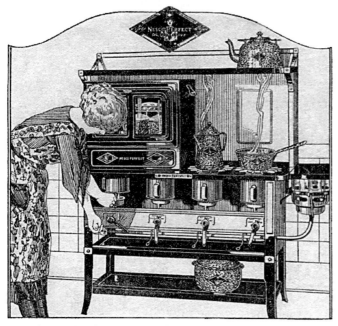

made. This time it was Tom's most welcome voice on the other end of the phone line, and his call was accepted by the happiest mother in the world. Tom was in town and coming home!

I guess it might seem funny or strange, the way we carried on with our coffee get-togethers, but for us it was a touching way of staying in touch with one another.

As we sat around the table with Tom, he said we should not have worried. He was sorry he couldn't let us know sooner that he was OK. He talked about his experiences calmly, as if they were something that happened every day. His soft approach was for Mom and Pop's benefit. Tom stayed home for several days before he returned to duty.

In 1943, at the age of 17, I followed my brothers into the service. It took a lot of persuading, but Mom finally consented. For no particular reason, I selected the Marines, and off

to boot camp I went. Now there were four stars on the banner in the front window.

After about eight weeks as a boot, I got a leave, and like my brothers before me, I called Mom when I got to town and asked her to put the coffee on. I had been waiting to do that for a number of years! At the first coffee break in my honor, so to speak, I finally had some experiences of my own to relate.

It was good to see Mom and Pop and my sisters. While Mom must have been torn with worry on the inside, she hardly let on. As she shared the pleasant time with the others, she added a few choice stories of her own, like the time Frank was showing off how he could fry eggs, flipping them in the air and catching them in the pan. Trouble was, one day he flipped the eggs into the air but missed them. That was bad enough, but he couldn't find them for some time. Seems they ended up out of sight, in one of Mom's shoes setting near the stove.

That was my one and only leave from the Marines. After special schooling, I shipped out for California and then Hawaii. I learned that my sister, Jo, had joined the Women's Army Corps. That meant that the banner in the front window now held five stars. My sister Martha was the only child at home. Frank was now in Europe, and Tom, John and I were in the Pacific.

Before long I became involved in the battle of Okinawa. A month or so after landing, I learned that my brother John was also there. I searched him out one day on the southern part of the island. What a glorious reunion we had! We were sure we'd never see each other until after the war, and we both thought how nice it would be to be home with everyone, enjoying coffee in the kitchen. We spent several very short hours together before I had to return to my company.

I was glad I got to see him; who knew? It might be for the last time. Things were still pretty rough. I thought, *If all of us get home in one piece, we'll be very lucky.* I didn't know how Frank was making out in Europe, and Tom had been in several battles already. I wondered where he was.

A couple of weeks later, while cleaning my rifle, I looked up and saw three guys coming toward me. I didn't think much of it until I looked again.

There was my brother John, there to repay my visit! He had a couple of friends with him. I didn't look at them too closely at first, but then I noticed a familiar face. Of all people! It was none other than Tom! I could hardly believe it! Here were three brothers, each in a different service, meeting in a combat zone! I got some time off and we spent the rest of the day together. It was quite a day for the three of us.

Not long after, the war came to an end. Each of us returned home. As each of us got into town, we called home and asked Mom to put the coffee on. I can't imagine just how much she worried through those war years. The safe returns of all five of us, one by one, had to be the biggest joy in her and Pop's lives.

Over the next nine years, all of us kids married, including me in 1948. I attended a radio school in New York City and hoped to become a radio announcer. As luck would have it, I never got a break until much later in life.

I had a variety of jobs over the years but nothing I really wanted as a lifelong career. When most of the men at a factory where I was working got laid off, I joined the Army. It was 1955; I had been out of the service for nine years. I was assigned to photography school in New Jersey. The family continued to have their coffee get-togethers whenever possible.

After about three years in the Army, having been stationed in the states, I re-enlisted and was assigned to Formosa (Taiwan). Before the trip, I was given a leave and, as usual, I called Mom and had her put some coffee on. That last visit home was one I'll never forget. Mom was not in the best of health, but her spirits were good. I was saddened by the fact that she couldn't get around like she wanted to.

She laughed with the others as John told about the time he was going out one night and, as he was running to his car, he leaped over a cat. But he made a mistake. It wasn't a cat—it was a skunk! Tom joined in and told how the skunk got John in midair, as he was jumping over it. John's evening was ruined.

Then Tom was reminded about the time Mom came into his bedroom. Seems Tom jokingly said something and, in jest, she threw her shoe at him. Tom ducked and her shoe went through the window. We all laughed, including Mom.

In a way, I hated to leave for overseas. I'd miss our coffee breaks and the crazy stories we had told for so long. And, of course, I'd miss Mom and Pop.

I continued to write home regularly. Mom had gotten worse and was living with Frank and his family. Pop was living with my sister Mary and her family.

I'd been there for about 16 months when, one Sunday morning, an M.P. came to my home in Formosa and told me that my mother was quite ill. He suggested I go home on emergency leave at once.

It shook me up. After making the necessary arrangements and getting my leave papers, I bid my wife goodbye and left for home. I landed in San Francisco and lined up my flight east.

I dialed my brother Frank's home, and he answered. I said, "Frank, this is Joe. Tell Mom to put the coffee on; I'm coming home. Maybe it will cheer her up a bit."

I heard nothing for what seemed like several minutes. Then Frank said, "I'm sorry, Joe, our coffee breaks with Mom and the family will never be the same. Mom passed away yesterday."

I was stunned! Both ends of the line were silent. "I'm on my way," I finally said. I had hoped the urgent message I received was overstating the seriousness of her condition. I wanted so much to get home, to see Mom and talk to her. I wanted to call her and ask her to put the coffee on, 'cause I was coming home. I wanted to hear her chuckle. I remembered her smile when any of the family came home. That's the way I want to remember her—my Mom, the best coffee hostess I've ever known. ◆

# In a
# Logging Camp

*By Lillian Baker*

It was in the early '20s, in fact, 1922, when my husband, Ed, was hired to cook for a crew of 40 men. He received the big salary of $200 a month. What's more, they hired me as a flunky for $150. We thought we had it made—$4,200 (no income tax) a year and "found" (board).

You know what a flunky does? She gets to peel the vegetables, wash the dishes, set up the tables, anything the cook doesn't want to do. The dishpan was about 6 feet by 8 feet by 4 feet deep, hewed from a big log. The water was heated on the iron stove which filled a space about 6 feet by 10 feet on one end of the cook shack. The cook shack was 150 feet by 50 feet, with long tables, and benches that held eight men each. Each table seated about 28 men.

Have you ever washed dishes for 50 people? Besides the loggers, there were the bosses' families. The bull cook packed the water in and out, scrubbed the floors, and took care of the bunkhouses where the men slept. He would lift the big kettles of hot water into the dishpan, then scald the clean dishes when they had been washed.

I would wipe the dishes and reset the tables for the next meal. Our alarm rang at 4:30 a.m. each morning, seven days a week. By 6 o'clock I was serving flapjacks, bacon and eggs. There were doughnuts or cinnamon rolls set on each table, and some kind of canned fruit.

The top of the stove was solid sheet iron, which was greased with bacon grease, and 20 6-inch flapjacks could be cooked at a time. The men had hearty appetites, and could stow away four or five large flapjacks, plus several thick slices of bacon, and eggs. Ed cut the bacon by hand the night before. The coffee boilers held about 10 gallons of coffee, and were always kept full throughout the day.

When the breakfast work was done, I would start my bread, eight or

10 loaves, and Ed would take a quarter of beef out of the cooler, a 10- by 16-foot building, with all sides open and covered with wire screening. It would hold one beef carcass, one hog, and many chickens, with a meat block in the center where Ed would cut the meat. A 30-pound roast was about right for dinner, plus steaks for supper.

While my bread was rising, I would make 10 pies for dinner. Berry pies were made from gallon cans of fruit; apple pies took a little longer!

My goodness, where did all the morning go? It's time to fix the vegetables while my pies are cooking. Guess we'll have to have baked taters today; there are 400 pounds in the commissary. I'll scrub 55 of the larger ones, and get them in the oven as soon as the pies are done. Then I'll open three gallon cans of string beans, and cook them with bacon.

There are light rolls left from yesterday, and a gallon can of sauerkraut. Ed can make soda biscuits for supper. Pies are enough for dessert. I'll just have time to knock down my bread, and put it in loaves so it'll be ready to go in the oven soon as dinner is over.

Ten minutes to noon, the men are washing up. Large gray granite washbasins serve the purpose, and large roller towels hang beside them. I'll ring the dinner triangles.

The men are hungry. They have been working since 7 a.m. in the forest, on the end of a crosscut saw.

You never saw a crosscut saw? Well, it's about 8 or 10 feet long, with deep teeth that make a smooth cut to topple the tallest tree in the forest. When the timber is down, it is cut in log lengths. Men with sharp axes trim off all the limbs.

Two horses stand ready to haul the logs from the woods. They are hitched to a doubletree with a huge iron chain attached to an iron tong, somewhat like pinchers. The sharp spiked ends bite into each log. This is called a cant hook; why, I don't know, because it *can* hook or hold the log. It is then skidded to a pile, where two men with peevees stack them until they look like a small mountain.

There they wait the coming snow, when they will be loaded onto sleighs and hauled to the river bank until the ice melts in the spring. Again, the skidding cant hooks and peevees will move the logs to the river, to float to the mills where the logs will be cut, planed, and made into lumber. Wouldn't it be simpler to build log houses? *This* is progress?

Guess I'd better get back to the cook shack before my bread burns! There's supper to think about. I must make two big cakes, and Ed will have his doughnuts ready for me to fry in the big iron kettle of hot lard. How many? Let's see, the boys generally take two at a time with their coffee and come back for more. If we make a big batch, like 600, we won't have to make any tomorrow.

The days are getting pretty warm. Air conditioning—what's that? This is 1922, remember? The doughnuts are done. We'd better think about supper. We'll have boiled navy beans, fried taters and onions, rutabaga with butter, hot biscuits, pork chops and milk gravy, doughnuts and cake for dessert. I'd best scrub a big kettle of small spuds and cook them with their hides on so the boys can have hash browns with breakfast. Should go right nice with sausage and flapjacks.

The days are long, from 4:30 a.m. till 8 at night, but we must still go home and get vegetables for the next day and dig ice for the icebox. This we had put up last winter in out big icehouse. Ice blocks 18 inches by 18 inches by 20 inches were packed on all sides with sawdust hauled from the sawmill, where our logs will go. Little did we know that the ice and many vegetables in our root cellar would be

*Two men stack the logs until they look like a small mountain. There they wait the coming snow.*

used in a logging camp. This saved a 25-mile trip to go for supplies as long as they lasted. We were paid extra for these.

The evenings were long for the men, and were spent gassing and telling stories. Many times our daughter and the bosses' children were wide-eyed listeners. Sometimes the little girls would sing for them. One evening as we were busy in the cook shack, we heard the men laughing and clapping as if they were being entertained. This went on for several evenings.

One night Nedra came in with some nickels and dimes in her hand. I asked her where she got them, and she said the men gave them to her when she danced for them. Needless to say, there was no more dancing, and no more money, thus ending what might have been a promising career in show biz! Nedra was a very unhappy little girl for a while, but soon returned to the cheerful little girl everyone enjoyed once again.

Late fall and the snowflakes began to fall. Some of the married men had gone home, waiting for the time of deep snow when the logs could be hauled to the riverside. Thanksgiving came, and we cooked the usual dinner—turkey and stuffing. We had no sweet taters so we baked the white ones. And we had cranberry

sauce, yellow squash, baked beans, hot rolls, mince and pumpkin pie. Days when the men couldn't work they went hunting, so we had two saddles of venison roasted to go along with leftover turkey. Also, I had made a large kettle of vegetable soup, and for dessert there was hot gingerbread with whipped cream and spicy cupcakes.

Then came the spring thaw. The ice on the river cracked and buckled; there was water on top of the ice. The warm winds and rain melted the ice and it floated down the river. The water got higher. The logs along the bank were rolled into the river and floated down to the mills. The logs left in the forest were added to those already on the riverbank.

The entire logging crew came back to finish the job. (Jobs were hard to find in those days.) The crew cleaned up the forest, piled branches and burned them. The forest was always left in good order. This took about a month.

After a final celebration dinner of roast beef, fried trout (caught by the men in their spare time), baked beans, scalloped potatoes or potato salad, rutabagas, corn bread or hot rolls, pickles, jellies, hot apple pies and molasses cookies, there were goodbyes and many thanks for the good grub the men had enjoyed. We were given all the supplies from the cook shack, which amounted to many months of groceries for our family. We returned to our ranch about 10 miles below the camp.

So ended an event in our lives, long treasured and remembered. ◆

### Lumberjack Beans

3 slices bacon, cut into pieces
2 onions, finely chopped
1 teaspoon salt
½ teaspoon pepper
1-pound can stewed tomatoes
1-pound can red kidney beans
Heat oven to 150 degrees. Combine all ingredients and pour into a loaf pan. Bake for 1 hour. It's good!

—*Mrs. Josie Schrader*

# Custard's Calamity

### By Ethlyn Alsop Pastrone

Marie was 5 and the next to youngest of seven children. When baking custard pies, her mother always made a 4-inch pie for Marie, for of all life's values, custard ranked first with Marie. One time the mother did not have enough dough left to make a 4-inch pie; she used a jar lid and made a smaller one.

Marie cried, for there was less pie. The mother vowed she would never make another 4-inch pie for Marie, for Marie was becoming spoiled and was big enough now to eat pie as the others did.

Some time after this, the mother made two large pies and put them on the pantry shelf to cool for dinner. Later she went into the pantry and saw only the shell; someone had eaten the custard off the pies. Marie faced third-degree questioning.

"Maybe the kitty did it," she kept saying, and ducked her head and cried.

Next morning her father took her on his knee and told her how wrong it was to lie. "You tell the truth," he said, "or you will be spanked."

Finally Marie admitted that she had eaten the custard off the pies, but that did not settle things. Her older brothers and sisters teased her forever, called her "Custard." It was, "Custard, do the dishes"; "Custard, pass the salt"; "Oh Custard, do you remember that time?"

Thirty years later the seven children—all teachers now—gathered from four states to spend Christmas with the mother. (The father had died a few years after the custard pie episode.) During this vacation, the mother had custard pie for dinner. This set the family to teasing again.

This time Marie flared up. "Well, I'm too big to spank for telling the truth. You can all think of me as a liar along with your thoughts of thief, but I did not eat the custard off those pies! Now swallow *that* truth!"

Two of the older sisters winked at each other. One of them said, "Well, we are too old also to be spanked for telling the truth now; we did it and felt safe, for when asked, each could say, 'No,' for each ate only half."

There was quite a silence. Then the mother said, "Why, why, girls, and all that time? If I were a bit stronger, you would both get it yet!"

The day before leaving, Marie saw a 4-inch custard pie at her plate. Did the mother break her vow? Did the sisters repent?

Now Marie is only her middle name, and it has never been used—except once, when she wrote a true short story for *Good Old Days*. ◆

### Great-Great-Grandma's Baked Custard

1 pint whole milk
2 large *or* 3 small eggs
2 tablespoons sugar
Pinch of salt
½ teaspoon vanilla extract
Ground cinnamon *or* nutmeg

Preheat oven to 325 degrees. In a bowl, combine milk, eggs, sugar, salt and vanilla. Blend well, but do not beat air into it as this makes it coarse-grained.

Pour custard into a baking dish; sprinkle with ground cinnamon or nutmeg. Set dish in a large baking pan filled with hot water. Set pan in oven. Bake for about 1 hour, or until a silver knife inserted near the center comes out clean.

—*Jan Wehrlie*

# When Santa Asked Questions

*By P.J. Brown*

*I*n 1917, interest in health foods was not as prominent as it is now. Most families usually had some particular items they favored as "being good for you" and my mother felt that oatmeal porridge and brown bread were things we children should eat often.

When she was 5 years old, my sister disliked both the porridge and brown bread and had to be scolded into eating them. My mother was having more than the usual difficulty with her just before Christmas. In an effort to persuade my sister to conform with her wishes, Mother suggested that it might be a good idea if she did eat the two foods. If Santa Claus should come, he would ask her if she had been a good girl, and how was she going to say she was if she had to admit she was not eating her porridge and brown bread? My sister bragged that she wasn't afraid of Santa and that she would look him in the eye and tell him she *hadn't* eaten them, and nobody could make her!

Unknown to my sister, my parents planned to play a trick on her. And they had taken me, her 10-year-old brother, into their confidence. My father, who was very rotund and just the right build to impersonate jolly Saint Nick, had rented a Santa suit from a theatrical costumer. The suit really was a beautiful thing. The outfit included shiny, black leather boots, the traditional scarlet tunic, baggy breeches, mittens and a toque, all trimmed with real white fur. There was also a wide belt with polished brass buckle, and a wig, mustache and beard. The last three items were not the obviously artificial kind so many department-store and street-corner Santas wear today; they looked very much like human hair, and were attached with gum arabic, like actors use on the stage.

The day my father was to play Santa, my mother helped him prepare for his masquerade by reddening his nose and cheeks with greasepaint. He was a very imposing sight indeed! He had donned the trappings in the basement of our home and then made his way into the garden to hide in a playhouse we children had built among some trees. My sister, who was unaware of what was taking place, was inveigled into the kitchen by the pretext of showing her some birds busy in the feeder we always kept stocked with seeds and suet each winter. The window from which she was looking had a good view of the playhouse. To her utter amazement, out of it stepped Santa Claus, complete with a big pack on his back, and he began to trudge through the snow to our front door.

I don't think there was ever a more startled child than my sister. It must have flashed through her mind that she stood a very good chance of being questioned by Santa as Mother had predicted, for she squirmed out of my mother's arms and ran into the dining room where she hid behind the door. Santa pounded at our front door and was admitted with a great deal of laughter and "Ho, ho, ho's." Then he announced in a loud voice that according to his list, there was a little girl he should see.

In response to my mother's comment that she had no idea where my sister might be, Santa commenced to search the house room by room, leaving the one in which my quaking sister was hiding for last. Finally he "found" her. Of course, he asked her if she had been regularly eating her porridge and brown bread. Gone was the defiance she had been claiming she would show. With eyes as large as saucers and hardly able to speak, she managed to gulp that she *had*, terrified that if she told the truth, Santa might pass her by. Her knees were knocking together and her only concern was to be free of the presence of the awesome saint who bent over her seeking answers to his embarrassing questions.

Santa took pity on her and patted her on the head. He admonished her to keep eating the two foods she disliked but that were good for her, gave her a small present, and promised to do better by her at Christmas if she behaved herself. Then he left the house while my mother, our maid and I waved goodbye. But my sister, who was going to be so brave and face up to him, still stood trembling in her corner behind the door, thankful that she had managed to have her falsehood accepted by Santa.

My father made visits to several children in the neighborhood, asking each about his or her behavior (the questions having been prearranged by their parents). He gave each a small toy or some candy, and then made his

way home to divest himself of his costume in our garage.

The trick must have worked, for I remember my sister ate her porridge and brown bread with gusto through the remaining days before Christmas and for many weeks thereafter! I remember, too, that she retained her faith in Santa Claus long after her little friends lost theirs. No wonder; she had ample reason to believe he did exist! ◆

## Brown Bread

*This recipe was a favorite of Mrs. Robert S. Versey, wife of a former governor of South Dakota.*

    2 cups cornmeal
    1 cup flour
    1½ teaspoons baking soda
    1 teaspoon salt
    ½ cup molasses
    1 cup sweet milk
    2 cups sour milk

Sift together dry ingredients. Pour in molasses and milk. Beat hard and pour into a greased mold. Steam for 3 hours, and then dry in a hot oven for a few minutes. This mixture is very thin and makes a delicious bread.

—*Mrs. Marjorie Lawyer*

## Mrs. Randlet's Brown Bread

*This recipe was given to me in 1907, the year I was married.*

    1 cup cornmeal
    1 cup rye meal
    ½ cup molasses
    ½ cup sugar
    1 cup water
    1 teaspoon baking soda
    1 teaspoon salt
    1 cup raisins

Combine all ingredients; steam for 3 hours.

—*Mrs. Walter Downing*

# Mr. Thomas' Frog Dinner

*By Mel Tharp*

At my grandmother's house, cream day was something I looked forward to. In 1936, I spent most of the summer with my grandparents on their farm in western Kentucky. Each Wednesday was cream day and this meant a trip with my grandmother to Ike Johnson's grocery.

Ike ran a country store which wasn't much by modern standards. He carried the standard line of canned goods, cured meats, farm supplies and dry goods. Ike also bought poultry for the poultry houses. And he had a small cream-testing substation where his wife, Gladys, tested the cream for butterfat content. Ike, in turn, paid the prescribed market price, then shipped the cream on to the main creamery. A 5-gallon can of cream and a market basket of eggs bought a lot of groceries in those Depression years.

On this particular morning, I had turned the cream separator until my arm felt as if it would fall off. It was tiring work, but I felt that a trip to Ike's store was more than adequate compensation for my labor.

Suddenly, Grandma dashed my hopes by announcing that I would not be allowed to accompany her that afternoon. "Now don't be so upset," she said. I'm going with Millie Thomas. She's taking the truck. Effie Smith and several other women are going along, and by the time they get their cream and eggs in the truck, there just won't be enough room for you. You can stay over at Millie's house and play with Eleanor while we're gone."

The Thomas place adjoined my granddad's farm. Lawrence and Millie Thomas had a 7-year-old daughter named Eleanor whom I thought could play almost as well as a boy. She made a good cowboy pardner and we cleaned out a lot of holdup nests together. She also liked Jack Armstrong, and I knew that any girl who liked the All-American Boy couldn't be too bad, so I decided that my day wasn't to be a total loss after all.

Grandma and I walked over to the Thomas house where Millie and the other women were waiting, Millie making out her grocery list. "Lawrence," she called her husband. "Do you want anything from the store?"

"Nothing from the store," he replied, "but if you see the

Butler boys, tell them to bring me a mess of frog legs and I'll pay them. I ain't had a frog leg dinner all summer."

The women left for the store. As soon as they were out of sight, Mr. Thomas said he had some corn on the back part of the place that needed plowing. He told us to play around close to the house and gave us the usual admonition to be good children.

After Mr. Thomas left for the cornfield, we decided to play cowboys. I was the Lone Ranger and I wanted Eleanor to be Tonto, but she insisted on being Shirley Temple. We finally compromised on Little Orphan Annie. The Thomas apple orchard had some June apple trees laden with fruit. A tart June apple sprinkled with a dash of salt was just what we needed to get us ready for the trail. While reaching for an apple, I almost stepped on a toad. This planted the seed of what I thought was an excellent idea.

I suggested to Eleanor that we go frog hunting. I told her how pleased her dad would be when he came home to find a nice frog supper waiting for him. She agreed that it was an excellent idea. No one had told us toad frogs were not an edible species.

First we looked around for something to hold our captured game. Eleanor remembered her mother's 4-quart aluminum cooker. It had a top which fit snugly, so the cooker seemed made to order. The toads were not hard to find. The meadows and orchard were abundant with them, and it wasn't long before we had what we considered a sufficient number for Mr. Thomas' dinner. At first, we considered if we should clean them, but we decided against this since neither of us knew much about dressing frogs for the table. We thought it would surprise everyone even more if we just left them setting on the dining-room table.

We were playing out behind the stock barn when the ladies returned. So engrossed were we in bringing bad men to justice that we never realized they were back until we heard a bloodcurdling scream coming from the general direction of the Thomas kitchen. There were more screams; each seemed to gain in decibels. We ran to the house and burst into the kitchen

just as Effie Smith let out a shriek that would have caused the banshee to tuck his sheet and head for the next county.

She was standing on a chair surrounded by toads, and when she saw us, she yelled, "Watch those children! Those things are deadly poison! I read where a woman out in Arkansas got bit by one and she died in five minutes!"

The other women looked shocked. I think they were more afraid of Effie than they were of the toads.

I don't know where it would have ended if Mr. Thomas had not arrived on the scene. He had broken a clevis and came to the barn for a replacement. He heard the screams and came running, fearing the worse. He soon restored order admirably. He picked up a broom and simply swept the toads out the door. His ability to assume control seemed to have a reassuring effect on Effie, and the crisis was over.

Eleanor and I confessed to being the culprits. To say that we faced a hostile court would be putting it mildly. Mr. Thomas was great in our defense, however, we were let off with a severe tongue-lashing. He explained the difference between toads and bullfrogs. He said he understood that we meant well, but in the future, we should ask before jumping into something we weren't sure about. He also said that any reoccurrence of this sort of thing, and he would personally have our hides.

I have been on several frog hunts since that day. Most of my hunts have been more successful in terms of providing meat for the table. I'm sure, however, that I have never been on a more exciting one. ◆

# Homemade Bread

*By Georgia E. Chamberlain*

Today homemade bread is a treat. Years ago it was an everyday necessity. Every housewife set aside a day for making bread, and even when it became possible to purchase "bakery bread," as it was then called, the housewife considered herself remiss if she had to fall back on a loaf of it now and then.

Until I was 10 or 12 years old, my mother baked our bread. It was the most wonderful treat in the world—the heel of a warm loaf, spread with butter. And if there was applesauce to put on it, that was bliss.

My mother and father were married in 1894. They went to housekeeping on the second floor of a house that stood on the side of a hill. Their street ran west into a long hill that ran north and south.

*Thousands of culinary treats I have enjoyed in the past 70 years have never exceeded that warm end crust of bread.*

Mother did not buy yeast at the store. She made her own from potato water. It always puzzled me how such good bread could be made with potato water, which, in my estimation, did not have a very delightful odor.

Mother didn't think so either when she attempted her first batch of dough. In fact, she thought she had made some terrible mistake. She decided to discard the mixture and seek advice from someone who had more experience.

But what to do with the dough? Terribly disgruntled with the smelly batch, she decided to throw it over the side of the hill.

That evening, when Father came walking up the hill toward home, he saw huge blobs of something white on the face of the hill back of the house. The minute he got into the house he said to Mother, "Stella, come out and see the huge puffballs on the side of the hill."

Mother finally got used to the teasing about the discarded dough, and until she had been married 15 years or more, she made baking bread a weekly task.

No one has ever made better bread—large brown crusty loaves, usually six at a time. Just the thought of them makes my mouth water.

Many restaurants today serve small crusty loaves of homemade white bread with a meal, but they never quite come up to the taste of Mother's bread, which had none of today's preservatives, vitamins and enriched flour. Even my own loaves lack the taste Mother's had. ◆

### Irish Potato Rolls

1 potato, peeled and quartered
1 cake yeast
3 tablespoons sugar
4 cups flour
2 teaspoons salt
Walnut-size lump of shortening

Boil potato; remove potato from the pot but save the water. When it is lukewarm, dissolve in it the yeast cake and sugar. Let set while you mix flour, salt, the mashed potato and shortening. Then add yeast mixture. If this is not enough liquid to make a spongy dough, add more (I use about one cup of water for the boiling and usually have to add about another cup of tap water for the dough).

After kneading the dough, place it in a greased bowl and let rise. Make into rolls and let rise again. Bake in 475-degree oven.

### Rolled Oats Bread

1 coffee cup of rolled oats
1 tablespoon lard
1 pint boiling water
½ teaspoon salt
½ cup molasses
½ yeast cake dissolved in ½ cup warm water
Flour

In bowl, place rolled oats and lard; pour boiling water over it and stir until lard is melted and ingredients are combined.

In another small bowl, combine salt, molasses and dissolved yeast; stir into rolled oats mixture and blend to combine. Mix in flour to stiffen. Let rise overnight and continue as for yeast bread.

—*Mrs. Susan J. Winn*

### Sour-Milk Yeast Buns

1 cup sour milk
½ teaspoon baking soda
3 tablespoons sugar
½ teaspoon salt 
1 cake yeast softened in a little warm water
1 egg, beaten
4 tablespoons shortening, melted
1 teaspoon baking powder
5–6 cups flour

Thoroughly mix sour milk and baking soda, then add sugar, salt, and softened yeast. Next add beaten egg and melted shortening. Lastly, add baking powder and enough flour to make a rather firm dough.

Knead very little. Let rise in a warm place for 2 hours. Make into small, flat buns and place in a greased baking pan 1 inch apart. Let rise until double in bulk. Bake in a 400-degree oven for about 25 minutes, or until done. Makes 2 dozen.

The addition of raisins and a dash of cinnamon makes a bun that appeals especially to children. Use about a cup of seedless raisins, mixing them in after part of the flour has been added.

—*Mrs. C.A.B.*

# Thank Heaven For Biscuits!

*By Pauline Jensen*

ather's habit of bringing home unexpected guests for meals created many a crisis in our lives. When Mother chided him about it afterward, he always replied, "I knew you'd manage somehow."

But Mother's ingenuity came near to failing that rainy, chilly Sunday evening just prior to our entrance into World War I. Father had gone back to the grain elevator he operated, intending to finish up a few tasks left undone on Saturday. Tom, my brother, and I curled up on the braided rugs, our dog and cat between us, and listened as Mother read to us.

She had scarcely finished a dozen pages when the door burst open, and Father banged into the room followed by seven young men. Ushering them toward us, he said, "Fellows, meet my wife, Mary, and my children, Peggy and Tom."

*For a few minutes I had a pretty bad time. I wondered what on earth I'd feed a hungry crowd like that.*

Then he explained that en route home from the elevator, he noticed that the 7:40 passenger train bound for Omaha had pulled to the side tracks. Investigating, he learned that the engine had developed trouble, and that they'd sent to Omaha for repair parts.

"It'll be about three hours before they get rolling again," he said. He grinned at Mother. "These fellows are headed for Army camp. They haven't eaten since noon. They asked about a café, but since the only one in town is closed on Sundays, I invited them to come along with me. I knew you'd rustle up something for them to eat."

"We'd be glad to pay you," one of the boys chimed in.

The look of dismay on Mother's face disappeared. "Indeed not. You boys get comfortable in the other room, and the children and I will fix something for you. Nothing fancy, but enough to tide you over."

After they went into the parlor, Mother tied on her apron, and stood uncertainly in the middle of the room. I knew what she was thinking. We'd eaten every bit of the roast and finished off the apple pie a few hours earlier. Because of the muddy roads, Mrs. Wentzel had not been able to deliver our usual order of eggs and butter. Both of these items were in short supply. And with spring approaching, we'd used up the hams and bacon that hung from the attic rafters in the winter. Mother was in the most unusual circumstance of having little food on hand.

Suddenly her face brightened. "Tom, jack up that fire good so the oven will be hot." She pulled from the cupboards several of the four-loaf black tin bread pans. "Come with me to the cellar, Peggy," she said.

I followed, wondering what Mother had in mind. She scanned the shelves of canned goods. Quickly she reached for the two remaining tins of salmon, something we saved for special occasions. Then she loaded into my arms jars of spiced peaches and her choicest pears. From the jam cabinet she selected strawberry preserves, plum jelly, and a glass of amber honey. "Come, now," she urged, heading back toward the kitchen.

Tom had a crackling fire going. Mother yanked open the flour bin, and in her biggest crock, began mixing biscuit dough. "Set the table, Peggy—quickly!" she commanded. As I reached for the everyday dishes, she stopped me. "Use the good ones!"

In no time at all, it seemed, she had a pan of biscuits ready to pop into the oven, and a kettle of creamy white sauce bubbling on the stove. While the biscuits baked, she boned and drained the salmon and folded it gently into the simmering mixture. She cut another tin of biscuits, then filled the big tureen with the salmon sauce, sprinkling bits of parsley on it.

Father got the boys to the table, and Mother assigned the task of waiting to Tom and me. We watched, fascinated, as the boys attacked the food. Over split biscuits, they ladled the fragrant salmon. Other biscuits they piled high with golden honey, ruby jelly or rosy preserves.

The biscuits disappeared with unbelievable speed. Tom and I made countless trips to the kitchen for refilled plates. Each time we entered the room, Mother was either taking out of the oven a pan of the feathery things, or putting another tin in to bake.

The boys topped their meal with pear sauce, and

biscuits dripping butter. I held my breath. The butter plate was nearly empty, and there was no reserve.

Finally, several of them pushed back their chairs. One of them groaned, "I've never had a better meal in my life." He turned apologetically to Mother. "We ate like we were starved."

Mother smiled. "You were hungry! Boys always are!"

Later, after we'd seen them to the door and received their profuse thanks, Mother slumped wearily into the kitchen chair.

Father looked at her anxiously. "I hope it wasn't too much bringing those boys here to be fed. I kept thinking of where they were going, and I didn't have the heart to let them wait in the cold when they were hungry." He grinned. "Anyway, I knew you'd manage."

*Now,* I thought, *Mother will really give it to Father good. She'll tell him plenty, for bringing all those strangers here to eat the things she'd saved for special affairs.* I waited for her answer.

She sighed. "Poor boys! It was the only thing to do." She smiled. "For a few minutes I had a pretty bad time. I wondered what on earth I'd feed a hungry crowd like that. Well, it worked out fine!" Her laugh pealed out. "Thank heaven for biscuits!" ◆

# 10 Cents' Worth Of Ginger

*By Ethel A. Little*

Back in the early '20s, the hustle and bustle of Saturday morning on the farm included such chores as scrubbing floors, baking, sweeping the porches, filling the wood box, and dusting the parlor. You can guess that I, 6 years old, was assigned the most menial and boring—filling the woodbox.

As I plunked the last armful of wood into the box outside the back door, I heard my mother call from the kitchen, "Is there anyone around (I had a brother and six sisters) to go to the store for me—I'm out of…"

I darted through the screen door, letting it bang loudly. "I will, I will!" I shouted.

"No, you're not old enough to handle money," said my mother as she continued kneading the large pan of bread. "Get your brother at the barn."

It must have been my tearful look that moved her to say as she looked up from the bread kneading, "Well, all right; you may go. Get the money jar from the cupboard and take out a dime."

Amid a profusion of instructions from my mother regarding rules of safety along the road to the store and politeness to the storekeeper, I was off on my first trip alone to the country store. Down the hill I scurried, my bare feet raising their own dust storm along the edge of the road. Fearing that it would slip out, I stopped occasionally to

check the thin dime in my black patent-leather coin purse. It was such a good, grown-up feeling to be on this little business trip.

I stopped on the bridge at the foot of the hill to check Old Whiskers, the catfish in the creek below who had been eluding my father's hook for two years. I hurried on, remembering my mother's admonition not to loiter.

Around the bend, a lush patch of calamus grew so near the road that it brushed my skirts. Emerald green blades waved in the breeze as if beckoning me to stop for a taste of their sweet roots. There was no time for pulling calamus roots that day, and besides, I'd rather wait for the gingerbread that my mother was going to bake when I returned.

I was nearing the end of my quarter-mile journey and soon found myself in front of Elias Frey's General Store. The store was kept for the convenience of the surrounding farming community. I'm sure that Mr. Elias Frey, a farmer himself, made little profit. The store was not open during daylight hours except when a customer appeared on the porch of the store and

Elias saw him from his house, barn or yard about 500 yards away.

The store was a small, one-story structure, weather-boarded and paint-shy, with a sagging front porch approachable by one step. The step was a 6-foot plank laid on two rocks, one at each end. The plank wobbled as I hopped on it, so I quickly stepped to the firmer support of the porch.

***I was nearing the end of my quarter-mile journey and soon found myself in front of the general store. The store was kept for the convenience of the surrounding farming community.***

I was lucky; Mr. Frey was working in his yard, noticed me on the store porch, went to the house to get his money box and came slowly (he was 85) but directly to the store. After exchanging greetings and remarks about the hot day, I followed the cigar-smoking proprietor through the doorway.

The door was an ordinary one, well-worn, matching the rest of the building in its shabbiness, but was almost completely covered by a gaudy sign. The sign pictured a stern-faced, very red Indian with a multicolored headdress. Below him in bold, black lettering, I read (a newly acquired skill), "*RED MAN CHEWING TOBACCO.*"

I blinked rapidly as I entered the stuffy storeroom, trying to adjust my vision from the stark white sunlight to the almost pitch-black interior.

My nose was equally unprepared for the change from the fresh country air to the thick, unidentifiable odor emanating from within. Mr. Frey pulled the chain of the one-bulb light suspended from the middle of the ceiling and I immediately learned the sources of the mixed aromas. There was a tar smell from the rope on the shelf, lavender from the box of bath soap, kerosene from a tank with a leaking spigot and stale cigar smoke from an ashtray on the counter.

While Mr. Frey thumped and banged to get the lone window open, I stood there, deciding

that the whole scene was dull and unexciting. Suddenly the swinging light bulb cast intermittent shadows on something shiny off to my left; it was the candy case. For a moment I stood there, feasting my eyes on its contents.

Between the rounded glass front and the sliding glass doors of the back of the case, there were satiny brown chocolates in pleated paper cups, and in neat stacks, red-and-white striped candy sticks, definitely peppermint, beside sedate black ones, definitely licorice. Next to these a crystal plate held a pyramid of frosty white, raggedy coconut mounds.

On top of the case rested a glass candy jar filled with penny candy. I crept closer and peered at its contents. There were root beer barrels, chewy caramels, candy "bacon" strips and little green candies shaped like watermelons.

I thought, *Oh, why didn't I asked my mother for just one penny?*

Mr. Frey startled me, though he spoke gently. "Now may I help you, dear?"

I quickly turned my attention and my body—salivary glands, taste buds and all—from the unattainable items in candyland to the reality of the moment. The gentle, bespectacled storekeeper stood behind his neat wainscoted counter with its cash box, scales and wooden spice boxes, ready for my order.

"Ten cents' worth of ginger, please," I sighed. ◆

### Gingersnaps

*This recipe was written for my mother by a neighbor, Mrs. C.J. Murray, and is dated May 7, 1897. Mother used it when I was a child, and I have the recipe paper given to her by Mrs. Murray.*

1 cup molasses
½ cup sugar
1 cup butter
1 tablespoon vinegar
2 tablespoons warm water
1 teaspoon baking soda
Flour to mix so can pat out in hand
1 tablespoon ginger
No mixing instructions are given.

—*Nina Corwin*

# *Jessie*

*By Ruth Carpenter*

My older sister Jessie is the best cook in the family. An invitation to her table conjures up visions of chicken fried to golden perfection, or a Pike's Peak roast falling in succulent slices, a tantalizing hint of garlic following the knife as it cuts. The gravy, red with paprika, graces creamy mounds of mashed potatoes—real potatoes. She can always find fresh green beans, whatever the season. She cooks them with salt pork or ham hock to a delicious glaze and even more delicious taste. But at family gatherings, someone always reminds her of one meal that was not a success.

Mama didn't like to cook, and from an early age, Jessie haunted the kitchen trying to perform her special magic. She used few recipes, and those only as springboards for her own ideas. She knew instinctively what would work and what wouldn't. When she was 13, Mama turned the cooking over to her, gladly cleaning up after meals in return for Jessie's fantastic food.

One Thanksgiving when Jessie was about 18, we invited cousins from a small town 40 miles away to come to dinner. At the crack of dawn, before anyone else was up, Jessie rousted me out of bed to help her.

She made corn-bread dressing before taking the turkey we had plucked the day before from the ice-box. She stuffed it, slathered it with a sauce of her own devising, and placed it in a blue enameled roaster with a high domed top.

Then she turned her attention to her pies. First, the tender crusts had their edges crimped by her deft fingers. Then came the pumpkin filling, smooth and golden. The completed pies went into the heated oven.

Meantime, I was washing and stringing green beans. When she took them from me, she dropped them into a large pot with a small amount of water and a ham bone. When they were bubbling to her satisfaction, she left the kitchen, reminding me to start the yeast rolls— my contribution to the dinner. When the dough was ready for its first rising, she returned to the kitchen in a clean dress covered by an apron. She had combed her hair and made up her face.

### *Mama didn't like to cook, and from an early age, Jessie haunted the kitchen trying to perform her special magic.*

She warned that breakfast would be skimpy, but it seemed no time before she had made coffee, fried ham and eggs. The pies, brown and beautiful, came out of the oven to make room for the biscuits which Daddy always said had to be tied down to keep them from flying off the plate. I remember looking for the strings when I was quite young. Jessie put the roaster into the oven as soon as the biscuits came out and assured us the turkey would be ready for a noon dinner.

After breakfast, I cleaned up the kitchen while Mama made the beds, straightened the house, and bullied Daddy into a suit.

Jessie set me to peeling a mountain of potatoes, scolding when I cut the peeling too thick. She covered the potatoes with cold water and set them aside.

At midmorning our guests arrived, exclaiming over the delightful kitchen smells. Mama and Cousin Lil disappeared into the bedroom, while Cousin August accepted a cigar from Daddy as they settled down in the living room. My brother Jim entertained the assorted youngsters after Jessie and I had greeted them.

At 11 a.m., Jessie cut the potatoes into chunks and put them in a pot to boil on the open gas burner. She checked her beans and took the cover off the roaster so the turkey could brown. I punched down my dough and

went to the dining room to set the table. I laid on the special-occasion white linen tablecloth and matching napkins, then took from the cabinet the good dishes we had washed the day before, and set them in place. The good silver— actually nickel—completed the setting.

Back in the kitchen, Jessie had coffee bubbling and she enlisted my help transferring the turkey from the roaster to a large platter, which I carried to the dining room and set it before Daddy's plate, beside the large carving knife. While Jessie made gravy, I put the rolls in the oven and started mashing the potatoes using a wooden masher. The gravy made, Jessie took over the potatoes, adding milk and a generous lump of butter, beating them until they stood in snowy peaks. While I carried them to the table, she dished up the beans and gravy. From the icebox, she took celery, washed and crisped the day before, and placed it on a long oval dish. She put fresh butter on a saucer, spooned pickles, olives and homemade plum preserves into dishes. Finally she took the rolls from the oven, putting them in a bowl and covering them with a clean napkin. She checked the table, making few changes in my settings, and then called everyone to dinner. Only I knew she held her breath until their gasps of appreciation told her everything was perfect.

Cousin August spoke grace, and then we ate, filling our plates again and again, until finally we protested we could not possibly want dessert. But Jessie smiled and told me to clear away the dinner plates while she returned to the kitchen. When I arrived she had already cut the pies into precise segments. I put them on plates while she took whipping cream from the icebox and began beating it with the hand eggbeater. A bit of sugar and a touch of vanilla completed her art. She dropped globs of cream on the pie, somehow making them fall into graceful swirls. Everyone wanted dessert after all.

Daddy could hardly wait for everyone to be served before he dug his fork into his pie, but the anticipation on his face changed suddenly to surprise. He took another tentative bite, glancing at Cousin Lil and Cousin August, who were chewing and swallowing politely, their faces carefully blank. Jim and the children

could not hide their shock. "Jessie," Daddy roared, "you forgot the sugar in these pies!"

Jessie was 80 years old when this was written and still the queen of any kitchen she entered. When we teased her about those pies she always smiled.

"I'm just human, after all," she said, and we're thankful. ◆

### Grandmother's Squash Pie

1 cup maple sugar *or* 1 cup brown sugar mixed with 1 teaspoon maple flavoring

2 cups cooked, strained squash, pumpkin, sweet potato *or* carrots

4 eggs

2 teaspoons ground allspice

2 cups milk

1 teaspoon butter

2 teaspoons ground ginger

2 unbaked pie shells

Dissolve maple sugar or flavored brown sugar in a little water; stir in strained squash.

Add eggs, allspice, milk and butter; blend well. Stir in ground ginger. Divide between unbaked pie shells and bake until set.

*—Mrs. L. Phillips*

# Bakers Three

*By Alan Sanderson*

Retreating in my mind 40 years, I see a little boy being bundled up by his mother so he might go outside. He wants to help his dad rescue the family sedan from 3-foot drifts of new snow. Of course, the boy unknowingly gets in the way much more than he helps. With his little shovel he mounts a furious attack on the waves of winter wonderland. Eventually his arms grow tired. He pauses to rest and feels gusts of bitter wind flay his shivering body. His dad smiles encouragingly, but neither that nor the dazzling sun above warms him.

Suddenly the front door opens, framing his mother, holding a platter of hot, homemade gingerbread. Father and son drop their shovels and run for the source of the honeyed aroma blown about in the frigid air. What a delicious treat! What a poignant memory! It was loving gesture repeated many times by my mom while I was growing up. Because I treasure this bygone scene so dearly, I cannot begin to think of her scented kitchen without first remembering and savoring to the fullest those gingerbread days.

*I cannot begin to think of my mother's scented kitchen without first remembering and savoring to the fullest those gingerbread days.*

As the years passed, I continued to eat up the specialties of the house faster than my mom could bake them. Every Wednesday she'd bring out the old wooden rolling pin my dad had carved for her and make pastry. I used to enjoy watching her sprinkle flour on the big ball and patiently roll it out to the thickness of a small mat. She'd make enough for two apple or blueberry pies, a jam pastry and two muffin trays of tarts. These last delicacies were not only inlaid with my favorite grape jelly, but their recessed bottoms were crisscrossed with two thin strips of dough. Before I bit into a finished tart, it was a habit of mine to pluck these innards out first for eating.

That wasn't all she'd fix. There'd be the usual pan of gingerbread, some oatmeal cookies and a layer cake. Since the cake was the last to be eaten, she'd often get around to topping it off with frosting. Saturday morning was the ideal time. Then out would come the confectioners' sugar, a few pats of butter, the vanilla flavoring bottle, and a pot of heated water for blending these ingredients. In a jiffy she'd have the

desired composition and would be icing the cake with deft strokes from the blade of a table knife. Patiently I'd stand by her side, watching and waiting not so much for a piece of cake, but to scrape the frosting pan cleaner than when it had been taken from the cupboard.

Because our neighbors were spaced far and wide while we were establishing ourselves at a new address, many more opportunities to watch my mom turn out these goodies presented

themselves. I began to rightly anticipate each step of the recipe. Before long, I was asking to make a cake by myself. Her ready consent surprised me, but she was no doubt casting an eye toward the distant future when I might have to be totally self-reliant.

Two cups of flour were doled out for me to run through the sifter. Why, I don't know to this day; sifted or not, flour always appeared the same to me. In succession came the required amounts of baking powder, sugar, milk and shortening. These I dropped into a large white bowl holding two eggs. Then came the actual labor.

Using a wooden spoon from the silverware drawer, I was to tip the dish on its side and furiously whip these components into a homogenous batter. As I reluctantly understood it, the better the beat, the tastier the texture that would be created. At the stage where I thought

my arm should have the benefit of a sling, I was allowed to grease the cake pan with the aid of some waxed paper. Onto this thin film I'd add a coating of flour by shaking a pinch around the pan. I'd pour in the batter as evenly as possible, since moving the mixture about afterward was a definite no-no. A moderate oven was 350 degrees according to my mom. Forty-five minutes was generally consumed to bake these efforts of mine. I inserted a knife into the center to see if it was done.

My first finished product was a limited success. It fell, but that didn't alter the taste. Sequels had a dip to them, too, although I was very careful not to bang about during the crucial three-quarters of an hour. For some strange reason, I could only effect the desired rise when I employed a rectangular loaf pan. However, that was a minor quirk. I could bake, which was the important thing.

Pies and cookies followed. The training came in handy much sooner than anyone had expected. Due my grandmother's illness, my mom was away from home for a few months. I thought my dad would be delighted that I could also put sweets in the bread box. Such was not the case. He complained about my eating them before he could get there.

I looked forward to this culinary diversion all through the summer of 1946. My growing affinity for the kitchen must've shown rather plainly, as it attracted my 4-year-old brother, Mike.

Another pair of hands (and dirty ones at that!) in the tiny cooking area wasn't something we welcomed. Yet, the youngest member of the family wouldn't be denied short of a good cry and a spanking, so my mom gave him some throw-away scraps of pastry to roll around on the enamel-topped table. Seemingly placated, he began to join us every Wednesday afternoon. Then he started to notice that we were doing more with our dough than merely making grimy balls of it. We were told quite pointedly that he could make tarts as well as anyone else. It was either the threat of the disciplinary rod brought about by the threat of a whimpering protest, or a third muffin tin had to appear. The latter prevailed and the family peace was prolonged.

My brother was permitted a spoonful of jelly

to distribute as he wished amongst his tarts. My mom stood firm, though, when Mike asked to put them in her oven. As a result, he decided to do his baking over the hot-air grate in the kitchen floor. It must have seemed a crackerjack idea to him; he'd felt the heat rise from these openings on frequent occasions. While the two of us finished up and subsequently went about our other business, Mike went out to play.

Serenity reigned for an hour or more. It was shattered by shrieks of wall-to-wall anger and the stamping of pistonlike feet. Hoping that no accident had befallen my brother, we rushed to the source of the screams. Mike, convulsed by heartbroken sobs, pointed to the empty muffin tray. Everyone had completely forgotten about our pet Irish terrier who'd gulped the tarts down, dirt and all. Mike could not fathom such heartlessness, but since our dog had always understood that anything on the floor was hers, she was the picture of a puzzle as Mike chased her into the parlor, threatening bodily harm. Fortunately, my mom caught his arm and brought an end to this fiasco by administering the long-deserved spanking.

This incident brought an end to the bumpy trials of the bakers three. I went to school, and the following summer, to work. Thereafter, the bulk of my mom's baking was done while my brother served a sentence of an afternoon nap. He may not have gone far in the kitchen, but he did come to know, like me, the joys of hot gingerbread on a snowy day. ◆

### Mama's Gingerbread

*This recipe for gingerbread is over 100 years old. We all enjoyed it when we were children and know you will, too.*

1 cup sugar
1/2 cup molasses
1/4 cup shortening (I use oil)
1/2 teaspoon ginger
1 teaspoon cinnamon
1 teaspoon cloves
1 teaspoon cloves

1 teaspoon soda (dissolved in 1 teaspoon of hot water.)
2 1/2 cups flour
3 eggs, well beaten

Stir altogether, add to above ingredients, and mix well. Add flour to the other ingredients. Add eggs, the last thing before baking. (Mixture will be thin.)

Bake at 350 degrees or until cake springs back, about 45 minutes.

### My Grandma Cooley's Oatmeal Cookies

1½ cups brown sugar
½ cup Crisco or other shortening
2 eggs
2½ cups flour
1 teaspoon baking soda
1 cup sour milk
2 cups oatmeal
1 cup chopped raisins
½ cup chopped nuts
Preheat oven to 350 degrees.

Cream brown sugar and shortening together. Add eggs, one at a time, and beat well. Sift together flour, baking soda and salt; add to batter alternately with sour milk. Stir in oatmeal, raisins and nuts.

Drop on greased cookie sheet by spoonfuls and bake until brown.

—*Mrs. Earl Wilhelm*

# Birthday Bologna

*By Anna-Margaret O'Sullivan*

The September air blew in silky gusts and the sun threw lacy patterns under the trees. Treetops began to turn red and gold, and we knew fall was coming. With autumn came my eagerly awaited birthday. In our household, all birthdays were a time of joy and suspense. The Birthday Child—in this instance, me!—came upon whispering conspirators, who drew apart with secretive, tantalizing smiles. Rustling parcels were whisked under cover when I came into a room. As the great day drew closer, I fizzed with excitement.

My brother teased me with broad hints concerning the surprise he had for me.

"It's got pink roses on it. Don't you wish you knew what it was?"

"Some of it is round and flat. It's something you like, but don't ask me, I won't tell!"

I knew what it was. Every Christmas and birthday, he got me a set of little tin doll dishes. The only thing that varied was the color. One time it was pink, the next blue. But I played the game, pretending to be mystified and agog.

The Birthday Child had the privilege of choosing the kind of cake Mother would make. This year, after much pondering, I chose chocolate with chocolate icing. Mother told Bobo (which was our name for our grandmother) that she had read a new recipe for foolproof icing.

"You just melt chocolate creams in a double boiler and spread it over the cake," she said happily. "It can't fail."

Chocolate creams cost 10 cents a pound—even we could afford them. Sure enough, the recipe worked and on Sept. 30, the cake sat on the kitchen table in all its glossy dark splendor. At dinnertime, it would be topped with 10 blazing candles, the 10th being the "one to grow on."

If I could blow them out with one breath, I would get my wish.

At our family birthday dinners, Mother always lit the candles a second time for everybody else to blow out. It was never quite clear to me whether or not there was a second wish hovering about, but all of us wanted the candles lit again. We were always still laughing when the cake was cut and the blissful Birthday Child received the first piece.

Every September I was the B.C. and I reveled in unaccustomed importance. Only once a year was I so special that everyone deferred to me.

Besides choosing the cake, the privileged Birthday Child also chose the meat for the birthday dinner. My choice became a family joke and was repeated forever amid gales of laughter. I never lived it down.

"Bologna!" I said promptly. "I want bologna and bologna gravy."

*The Birthday Child had the privilege of choosing the kind of cake Mother would make. This year, after much pondering, I chose chocolate with chocolate icing.*

"Bologna!" Mother's eyebrows went up. "Wouldn't you rather have pork chops?"

"No, I want bologna."

She couldn't believe it. "Then how about chicken?"

"No," I said, aggrieved. "We never have any good meat around here. I want bologna and bologna gravy for my birthday dinner."

Bologna it was, plus bologna gravy. Once a year the Birthday Child had the final say. I can still see that platter of delectable pink disks, lightly browned, and beside it, a bowl of rich, spicy gravy.

Dinner, ending with the cake ceremony, was one of the high points of the day. The other was the presentation of the birthday gifts. Ordinarily, we did not use the "front room" in which my grandmother had put her maroon-plush, wicker settee and matching chairs. My sister, brother and I were guiltily aware that children left dolls and toys lying about any old place. We were frequently reminded of it.

"I want one clean, orderly place in this house where, if I died, I could be laid out," Bobo said grimly.

I thought how awful it would be if my grandmother suddenly fell dead, and I had to snatch Carrol Jean or Rosaline from the red plush cushions before she could be laid out.

But the ban on children using the front room was lifted on birthdays and holidays. The whole family trooped in, everybody looking as bright-eyed and expectant as I felt. I had to leave while they hid my presents. When I was allowed back in and was told to start hunting, a chorus of, "Cold—cold—warm—hot! HOT!" led me to the hiding places.

And such loot! I found an Eversharp pencil, a notebook for my stories, a Hershey bar, the tin dishes from Carrol, a box of crayons and a coloring book ... and finally, in a long box slid under the couch, the most beautiful doll I had ever *seen,* let alone owned. Patricia had a delicate face, long curls to the shoulder, and blue eyes that opened and closed. Her kid body was jointed at shoulders, hips, knees and elbows. From the knees down, she had cute composition legs and feet, and from the elbows, china arms and exquisitely detailed hands.

There was more. A small, decorated wooden chest held clothes to fit her: dresses, petticoat, nightgown, a robe (which then we called a wrapper), panties, even a checked apron, everything the well-dressed doll might need. My sister told me excitedly which garments she had made. Mother had made most of them on my great-grandmother's old White sewing machine while I was at school. My grandmother had crocheted a red sweater and cap. Mrs. Giltner, the lady hired to help with the care of my invalid great-grandmother, had made Patricia a little wool coat with a pocket for a tiny handkerchief.

*Finally, in a long box slid under the couch, I found the most beautiful doll I had ever seen, let alone owned. She had a delicate face, long curls to the shoulder, and blue eyes that opened and closed.*

The day on which I got Patricia, whom I still cherish, glows in my memory. But far more important than the gifts—which, after all, are merely things—was the family spirit of joy and anticipation, of sharing. When I hear of parents hiring clowns or ponies or a professional to run a child's party, I think back to the olden days, when birthdays were so special they belonged to the whole family to be celebrated and savored for all the rest of time. For me, September 1928 is unforgettable, rising to the glittering peak of my one-of-a-kind birthday on the last day of the month. ◆

# The Pea-Soup Story

### By Pete Vincent as told to Elinore McCune

"Hey, you guys! Shut that door or we'll never get warm. You can bring in the rest of your stuff later!" I yelled. The door slammed as a dusting of dry snow blew into the room.

I'm an old man now, but about 60 years ago I was one of three 16-year-old boys who had the temerity to venture into the Maine wilderness during Christmas vacation to spend a week in a lake-side cottage which belonged to Rahl's parents.

During the past three summers Rahl, Eddie and I had spent two or three weeks at this cottage fishing, hiking, reading or just lazing around during weather which was pleasant in the daytime but crisp at night.

This time it was different. A bitter wind blew across the snow that had fallen intermittently for two days. It drifted against the cabin, the trees and the brush. My father had driven us up and helped us shovel a path between the lane and the back door, but had hurried to start back home before the early winter evening closed down. Although we wore parkas lined with sheepskin or cheap fur, we felt we were freezing.

We found kindling and firewood in the woodbox, and as soon as I had a blaze going in the old, black, cast-iron cookstove in the kitchen, we holed up in there and began stuffing old newspapers into the cracks between the planks that formed the sides of the cabin.

Soon the roaring fire warmed us enough that the other two boys brought in the rest of the supplies. We kept on our leather-uppers—heavy shoes with rubber soles and foot coverings, but topped with leather that reached halfway to our knees and laced with leather thongs through flat metal hooks. We shed our parkas, and I took off my red plaid mackinaw and draped it over the back of a chair where it sent up little puffs of wool-scented steam as it dried.

As usual on these expeditions, I had volunteered to plan menus, select the food, and do the cooking. I had soaked dried peas the night before and drained them to bring along with the other food so before long, we had a huge pot of pea soup. It was made the old-fashioned French way with salt pork and ham scraps, and it was delicious. Except for breakfasts, when we often had fish, we ate on this soup for two days. Then Rahl said he was sick of pea soup and would I please prepare something else while they went fishing?

To fish, he and Eddie used an ice spud and took turns cutting several holes in the ice which was sometimes as much as 22 inches deep. Then they set wooden tip-ups in the water, and when a fish took the hook a red cloth flag flipped up above the surface.

I started to make a boiled dinner of beef, potatoes, onions, carrots and turnips—but I had only one large pot. It was sitting on the floor about one-third full of soup that had frozen solid. I put it on the stove long enough for the soup to thaw around the edges. Opening the kitchen door, I pitched the lump of soup into a huge snowbank where it sank completely out of sight.

When the boys returned, my boiled dinner was ready, and we ate on it for two days. Then I made a pot of spaghetti. The last day of our trip the pot was again empty.

When we returned from our final hike, Eddie declared it was a shame we didn't have any more pea soup to warm us—it would taste mighty good right now.

Quietly slipping out, I found the shovel and probed around in the snowbank until I found that lump of soup. I smuggled it in, dropped it in the pot, and built up the fire.

That evening we feasted on pea soup again—and it tasted better than ever. ◆

# Mom's Pies

*By Martha Mae Raines*

It was family reunion time and as usual the house was worked on for days. "A place for everything and everything in its place" were Mom's favorite words, so we were all put to work. Not only was the house to be cleaned, but it was to stay that way. I must admit that by the day before the reunion, everything looked spotless.

Now it was time to do the cooking and baking. Everyone was excited, and smelling all the good things Mom was preparing fast added to it. By midafternoon Mom not only had the food prepared, but she had also baked 10 of her famous cream pies.

After cleaning the kitchen, she and Dad decided to go to town to pick up some things she had run out of while doing all the cooking. The three younger kids would go with them while sister Margie and I would stay home.

Before leaving for town, Mom carried all the pies upstairs and placed them on a table in the hall. Then, telling us to be sure to keep the back door closed so the chickens couldn't get in the house, and to be sure not to make a mess, they left.

I sat around for awhile and read. I'm not sure what Margie was doing; she had wandered off somewhere. After about an hour, Henry, the boy from down the road, came. He yelled through the door for me to come out and play. Making sure (I thought) the kitchen door was closed, I went out. We had played for about an hour when he decided he was thirsty. I told him to go in and get a glass of water, but to be sure and not mess up Mom's house. (Yep, those were my words.)

He had just had time to get in the house when I heard him yell, "Martha Mae, Martha Mae! Come quick!" As I ran, all I could think of was how could he have messed up Mom's clean house that fast. Up on the porch and through the front door I ran.

I was halfway through the front room before I saw it. There was Henry chasing a chicken all over the front room. There was the chicken with meringue and pudding all over its legs and feet, dripping it everywhere it ran. As he grabbed the chicken and threw it outside, I followed the tracks through the front room into the dining room, up the stairs, and right to the table where Mom had placed her pies.

Now tell me, how do you tell your mother that out of the 10 pies she had spent half the day fixing, a chicken just ran through nine of them and then ran through her clean house—with pudding feet to boot?

Well, I thought, *I will clean up the mess and spare her that much,* but before I could turn and head down the stairs, I heard Dad's car pull in the lane. When Mom came through the door, I was standing in the middle of the room.

As I started explaining, Mom started crying. Now, Mom's not an easy crier, but this was something that deserved tears. It was too late to make more pies, so as sister and I cleaned up the mess and Mom cried, Dad went to the company store and bought pies.

The next day we all went to the reunion without Mom's famous cream pies, but with a story that has made us laugh every time we think of reunions and cream pies. ◆

### Grandmother's Old-Fashioned Cream Pie
1 cup sugar
3 tablespoons flour

*Well, I thought, I will clean up the mess and spare her that much.*

Unbaked pie shell
Rich milk (half-and-half is good)
1 teaspoon lemon *or* vanilla extract
Preheat oven to 450 degrees.

Combine sugar and flour; place in unbaked pie shell. Fill crust with rich milk; stir in flavoring. Stir filling to combine milk with sugar-flour mixture.

Bake pie for 15 minutes until crust is set. Lower oven temperature to 300 degrees and bake for about 1 hour.

*Caramel Pie:* Substitute brown sugar for white and use only vanilla extract.

—*Esther Carp*

# My Favorite Storyteller

*By Ruth Cleghorn*

As a child we never had much money, though Daddy worked very hard to provide us with necessities. Luxuries were few and far between. But the love and laughter we shared inside the cozy, warm old house made up for the lack of material things.

Living on a farm, we had to walk about a quarter-mile to catch the school bus. Each evening Bob, Mike and I would race wildly up the long road. Bob and I would always leave Mike behind but would wait for him to catch up as we grew close to the old house. The curl of smoke reached out to us and the sweet smell of wood burning reminded us of the warmth and love within.

An old sheet-metal wood-burning heater stood in the living room and Mama always had sweet potatoes baking or roasting ears roasting, buried in the hot coals. After the hassle of removing coats and gloves, then warming out half-frozen hands by the glowing fire, Mama would carefully remove the goodies from the coals. While the sweet, warm taste of potatoes or corn warmed our insides, the warmth from Mama's love and caring warmed our hearts.

*Later, after supper, we settled down in front of the fire, anticipating the story Daddy would tell of his childhood.*

Later, after supper, we settled down in front of the fire, anticipating the story Daddy would tell of his childhood. We sat, eyes aglow, as Daddy began in his wonderful, funny dialogue.

"Granny raised pumpkins every year and when they got ready to pull, she'd store 'em under her bed to keep 'em from freezing 'til time for Thanksgiving and Christmas baking. One day," Daddy shuffled his feet and took a long draw on his cigarette, "Buster and me were up to our usual mischievous tricks when we heard Granny holler, 'Buuu-ster! Rooo-bert!' We knowed right then we had been caught red-handed and was in fer it fer sure.

"Well, Buster wan't quite as brave as me. He stayed to take his lickin'. While Granny was lickin' him good I took off and hid under the bed. Well, now, Granny wan't quite the dummy I thought." Daddy laughed with a fond grin on his face. "And it wan't long 'til I heard her a-coming. Now, Granny was a litty bitty woman and just about as round as she was tall, and when she was mad," Daddy paused and whistled, "she shook the whole house when she walked."

"'Robert!' she warned, 'come out from under that bed.' But I drew up just as close to the wall as I could get and stayed quiet as a mouse. 'Robert! I know you're under there.' Granny warned one more time, then whack! She licked the biggest punkin of all."

"*Boy,* I thought to myself, *I'm safe as a kitten snuggled up next to his mama,* and let out a holler. Granny whacked again and I hollered."

Daddy shuffled his feet, paused for a moment while he rolled another cigarette, then continued, that same fond grin on his face. "After a dozen or more whacks I decided it was enough, and came crawling out, bawling and begging, 'Granny, I'm sorry I run. I won't never do it no more. Please don't hit me no more!'"

"Well, Granny knew I'd learned my lesson and put the blackgum switch away. It was all I could do to keep from laughin' out loud 'til I got to the barn, then I busted loose rollin' in the hay, laughin' til I cried, how I'd outsmarted Granny.

"Well, when Thanksgiving come and Granny went to roll out her punkins they were all rotten. Granny never did figger out what made 'em rot, and I wa'nt 'bout to say nuthin'. Buster? Well, I was bigger 'n' he was and he wa'nt 'bout to say nuthin' neither. And he never did, not to the day he died."

Daddy still tells his stories, and although I've heard them hundreds of times, I am his most avid listener, crowding in among the grandchildren. As I've grown older, I've come to realize not all of Daddy's stories happened the way he tells them. But it doesn't matter. The memories and the love and laughter they bring to those who listen are very real. ◆

### Old-Time Pumpkin Cake

½ cup light brown sugar
½ teaspoon salt
½ cup shortening
2 beaten eggs

¼ cup milk
¾ cup mashed, cooked pumpkin
2 cups cake flour
1½ teaspoon pumpkin pie spice
2 teaspoons baking powder
Icing (recipe follows)
Preheat oven to 375 degrees.

Mix brown sugar, salt and shortening. Add eggs, milk and pumpkin. Mix well. Stir in flour, spice and baking powder. Beat for 2 minutes. Turn into two greased and floured 8-inch cake pans. Bake for 35 minutes. Frost with icing.

### Icing for Old-Time Pumpkin Cake

¼ cup soft butter
2½–3 cups pulverized sugar, divided
¾ teaspoon ground mace
½ teaspoon vanilla extract
1 beaten egg white
½ teaspoon milk

Beat butter and 1 cup sugar together. Stir in mace and vanilla. Add egg white, milk, and more sugar until thick enough to spread.

*—Mrs. Brice Hall*

# Just Put in Some

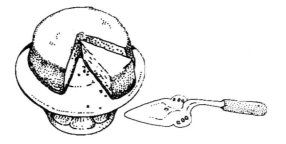

*By Anna-Margaret O'Sullivan*

A commonly held illusion about life in the good old days is that Mama, Grandmama, Great-Aunt Susie and old Mrs. Calabash across the alley all cooked superbly, by guess and by gosh, never measuring, but simply putting in a dab, a pinch, a handful, a sprinkle ... terms which may be summarized as *some*. If I had a quarter for every time I was told, "Just put in *some*!" I could make reservations for a leisurely cruise to the South Seas.

Some of these cooks might have enjoyed superb results with these methods, but it didn't always work like that.

In the 1920s and '30s, making a cake was a chancy undertaking. At our house during the cold weather, it had to be baked in the oven of a wood- or coal-burning range whose temperature was kept constant by some sort of legerdemain not perfectly understood by my mother or grandmother. In milder weather, we used a sort of tin box oven with racks which was set over two burners of a kerosene stove. Once in a while, air currents were precisely right (or we had a stroke of luck) and the thing baked. Otherwise, this oven either burned the bottoms of biscuits without browning the tops or browned the tops and left the bottoms white.

*When a cake was in progress, children were cautioned to stay out of the kitchen. If they had to go through, they were grimly admonished to tiptoe lest the cake fall.*

When a cake was in progress, children were cautioned to stay out of the kitchen. If they had to go through, they were grimly admonished to tiptoe lest the cake fall. I really cannot recall a time that the cake definitely fell; on average, Mother's cakes were so mediocre it was hard to tell. This never kept us from wolfing down every scrap, of course. We could have eaten our weight in sweets. But at ice-cream socials, anyone lucky enough to get a piece of Mrs. Gillespie's cake knew the difference.

In our kitchen, a cup was a cup. If at the time we didn't have an 8-ounce measuring cup, we used a 6-ounce teacup. As a fledgling cook, I had no idea there was a difference. This may explain some of the shortcomings in Mother's cakes since apparently she didn't either.

Our teaspoons were a lot closer to the standard measure than our cups. However, we also cooked with the traditional pinch of this, some of that, and a little of the other.

When I first learned to make fudge, I liked to have Mother close at hand to give advice at each step. One rainy day, she was busy in the other room but glanced in quickly at my cry of dismay.

"Mother!" I wailed. "The milk is blinky. It's starting to curdle!"

"Oh," said Mother consolingly, "it's not really sour, honey. Just put a little soda in it. I think it will be all right."

She went back into the dining room, and I stared frantically into the kettle.

"How much shall I put?" I called.

"Oh, a little; not much. Just put in *some*."

Blankly, I measured out a teaspoonful of soda and dumped it in. The mixture boiled up furiously. One spoonful seemed so tiny that I ladled another couple of spoonfuls. My fudge actually "fudged" in spite of the damp weather, but it was so bitter no one could eat it. "A little soda" was a completely different amount from "a little sugar"!

Incredible as it seems today, we used to beat egg whites into mounds of snowy fluff on a dinner plate using an ordinary fork. When at some point our family got a rotary eggbeater, all the cooks found it a marvelous labor-saving device.

In contrast to Mother's cake, my grandmother's pie was sheer ambrosia. Her piecrust crumbled at the touch of a fork and her lemon filling was fit for the diners on Mount Olympus. One would have supposed such a pastry cook would pass on her piecrust recipe to her only daughter, but the two of them failed to see eye to eye on a surprising number of things.

Whatever happened, it was always Mother's joke that she needed to bring the hatchet to the dinner table to cut her pie. This was sometimes almost literally true, till she started buying Betty Crocker crusts (which, of course, didn't compare with my grandmother's).

At rare intervals, very rare intervals, Mother's crust was a close second to Grandmother's. Trying to puzzle it out over the years, I gradually realized that Mother must sharply vary her proportion of shortening to flour from piecrust to piecrust.

On one of my visits home, we were in the kitchen, preparing to wash dishes using the big old dishpans I recalled from my childhood. Putting away a couple of half-eaten pies, Mother made her twinkling little joke about the hatchet. As an adult, I considered my piecrust one of my more successful efforts and I ventured a question.

"What recipe do you use, Mother? How much lard for each cup of flour? I have a recipe that is almost foolproof," I offered.

After a lifetime of erratic piecrusts, most of them tough, Mother waved the offer aside.

"Oh, I don't use a recipe," she said airily. "I just put in *some*."

We smiled at each other, washed up the dishes and, in complete understanding, never spoke of piecrust recipes again. ◆

# The Day Grandma Stopped Baking

*By Elizabeth C. Reinicke*

That was The Day!

The persistent noise of a horn honking irritated Grandma to exclaim, "I do believe this street is the noisiest in Indiana!"

Grandma was pouring and stirring sugar into a kettle of hot blackberry juice. Her small face was flushed from the heat in the big black range. Grandma's hair, once a soft gold, was full of long, white hairs. On humid days, as today, it curled around her face, but the large, round knot on top remained smoothly in place.

Her tongue made a clucking sound. "Liza, go look out front and see what in the world is going on!"

Obediently I skipped from the kitchen to the front door. On the street was parked a small panel truck, painted in a pretty sky blue. "Your Bakery" was painted on the side in large orange letters. The *honk! honk!* had been successful. The neighbors came all in a flurry and clustered around a tall, laughing man whose ample front was covered by a huge, white apron.

"Golly!" I exclaimed. "Grandma, come quick!"

Clutching a long-handled wooden spoon, she trotted through the house with short steps. "Whatever is this contraption?" Grandma wondered aloud.

"Go." She gave me a little push. "Hurry and pull the pan of jelly to the back of the stove."

By the time I did the errand and ran back, Grandma had removed her blackberry-stained apron. Grabbing my hand, she hurried us outside to join the others.

"Morning, Agnes," Grandma greeted her next-door neighbor. "Hi, Lou," she said to another.

"Oh, Hannah, my word!" Mrs. Plumle was breathless. "Have you ever seen such a thing?" She pointed a long finger at the truck.

"Come on," Grandma encouraged Miss Priscilla, as she hesitated at the edge of her lawn. Miss Priscilla was prim-pretty, an old maid, scared of her own shadow.

The bakery man rubbed his big hands together and cajoled, "Come now, friends, and peer into the magic door."

He lifted off white, waxed sheets of paper, exposing tray after tray of golden bakery goodies. The women chattered and pushed, licked their lips and *oohed* and *aahed*. No coaxing was needed.

The bakery man enticed, "Yeast doughnuts, plain and sugar-dipped. Cake doughnuts, iced with chocolate, with pink or white. Crullers that melt in your mouth. Pecan rolls, pineapple, peach, raspberry, apricot-topped—you name it, they're all there! Kuchens, full of plump raisins, cupcakes … here, half-pint, have a cupcake."

He teased, "Look at those blue eyes shine," as I shyly accepted a pink-iced sweet. He continued, "Rack on top holds light bread and all types of dinner rolls."

Grandma took a big breath, clasped her small hands in front of her like a child, and tilted her head way back to see eye-to-eye with the bakery man. "My good man, what is the price of these delectable-looking bakeries?"

"Not just delectable-looking, Ma'am, but delectable. Rolls and doughnuts the low price of 30 cents a dozen. Kuchens, 20 cents, cupcakes the same. Your Bakery will be here to serve you twice a week, Tuesdays and Saturdays. Our aim is to free you from hot kitchens in hot weather."

At Grandma's finger pointed upward, "Oh yes, the bread. Two loaves for 15 cents. Dinner rolls, dime a dozen. They are as tasty as your own, believe me."

Grandma's pretty eyes were full of excitement. "Run, Liza, fetch my change purse."

Loving every minute, she took her time choosing one dozen assorted pastries and two loaves of brown-topped bread. The two white paper sacks she handled gingerly were daringly larger than her neighbors'.

But the bakery man wasn't finished. From a large pocket in the apron he pulled out an order pad and with a flourish announced he had a surprise. Saturdays were special! Fruit pies were delivered to save the ladies baking on the Sabbath.

"Put one in the warming oven a short time and no one would believe it wasn't yours. Now,

friends, isn't that a break? It took Your Bakery to think of that!"

Grandma agreed. The neighbors shook their heads in the affirmative. As if mesmerized, the ladies tittered up at him and gave him pie orders for Saturday.

Successful in this block, the bakery man waved "Bye for now," and drove the sky-blue truck to the next block.

Grandma now had no time to waste. She left the chatter of the women and hurried us into the house. She tied on her apron, poked up the fire, pushed the pan of juice forward, put the teakettle on, and poured a small amount of barley soup into a saucepan.

"Liza, tear some lettuce for salad. You and I are going to have a bite and one of those delicious pastries with our tea. How's that?"

As if she didn't already know it would be fine with me! I shared Grandma's sweet tooth.

After our quick lunch, she motioned me to a small rocker without arms. Opposite it she pulled up her rocking chair. On a glass cake plate she handed me my choice—a scrumptious, chocolate-iced cruller. She eased herself onto the seat, right hand holding the cake plate carefully. She then set the plate on her knees and smiled down with childish satisfaction at her pecan roll, sticky with caramel syrup and a cluster of pecans. Grandma took a tiny bite, chewed daintily, then rolled her happy eyes heavenward. She motioned me to go ahead with my goody. We rocked, sipped hot tea, and took small bites until every morsel was gone.

That was The Day—the day Grandma stopped making light bread and rolls and doughnuts and …!

But, The Day hadn't ended.

Grandpa's arrival home from his job in the evening was routine. He would get off the 5:40 p.m. streetcar, slowly walk the two blocks home, step through the back door, set his dented black lunch bucket on the round, worn oak table and say, "Evening, Hannah. Have a nice day?"

That particular evening Grandma nodded pleasantly and waved her small hand toward the seven glasses full of purple-black jelly ringed with paraffin. Grandpa smacked his lips and smiled at me.

While Grandpa washed up for supper, Grandma covered the table with a green tablecloth, faded but clean and starched. She placed in the center a low white bowl holding sweet-smelling red roses.

Grandpa sat down in his chair, took a sip of grape wine, dabbed his mustached and inquired, "Company?"

"No," said Grandma, and called Aunt Mabel. Mabel was the last of my grandparents' children, a senior in high school.

The naked chicken had been dressed with lemon butter and sage, baked to a golden brown; it was placed before Grandpa on a thick, brown platter. The large bowl of home-canned green beans was ringed with potato halves. The glass relish dish was full of home-canned bread-and-butter pickles. Grandpa's tired face lit up. His favorite meal!

A whiff of hot light bread always commanded Grandpa's attention. Grandma placed the loaf of bread on its cutting board in front of him and handed him a knife. He always sliced the bread because, as he put it, "his womenfolk cut it too thin, trying to be society."

Grandpa poised the knife. "Smaller loaf, eh? How come?"

Grandma was sitting very straight. Her eyelids lowered briefly, then her blue-grey eyes looked directly into Grandpa's brown ones. "A new and modern thing came to our neighborhood today. A bakery on wheels! I bought two loaves."

"Hmm. How much?"

"Two loaves for 15 cents."

"Hmm." The head of this house commenced eating and we followed. After a few moments, "Hannah, how many loaves of light bread do you get from a 24-pound sack of flour?" he quizzed.

"How should I know?" she answered with a slight shrug.

Grandpa laid down his fork. "Who should know better than you? I'd say you've made thousands of loaves over the years."

"Ten thousand times ten thousand," corrected his wife. "That is why I'm going to stop making light bread and rolls and doughnuts and whatever else! I'm sure it is just as cheap boughten from the bakery truck. After baking for a family of 11 children for 36 years, why...." She gave another shrug.

Aunt Mabel shut her eyes tight and in a mock reverent voice said, *"Dieu vous garde* (God protect you),"* showing off her French.

Grandpa peered sternly at her over his horn-rimmed glasses. "That's enough."

"Oh, go ahead and finish eating while the food is still fresh tasting," urged Grandma.

Grandpa had a thoughtful look on his face, kinda like when he was pondering his Sunday-school lesson.

The delicious meal was topped with small bowls of home-canned peaches, cool from the cellar. Grandma removed the pastries from the warming oven, arranged them on a cake stand, and offered the colorful array to Grandpa first. I thought he was going to refuse, but he chose a round, fat doughnut, sprinkled with sugar and cinnamon.

Aunt Mabel licked her fingers, getting all the gooey from the cherry-topped Danish she had chosen. Grandma quietly poured each a cup of hot tea and helped herself to a pecan roll. This roll wasn't being enjoyed as the luncheon one was, I could tell. The silence was casting a chill over the dessert.

Finally, "From the bakery on wheels?"

"Yes, Mr. Clyde."

"How much?"

"Thirty cents a dozen, 15 a half-dozen."

Grandpa eyed the remaining six. "And you purchased 10 for the four of us?"

"Twelve," the word spat out. Dare he ask where the other two went? I'd never heard Grandma "talk back" to Grandpa in all my 12 years.

"Mr. Clyde, I've received the age of 54. Not old-old, but old enough. I have been a dutiful wife and mother. So help me," she said, raising her right hand, "this is the day I stop all that baking and sweating and hustling around. I'm going to start being a little selfish and a little lazy and ... oh, whatever!"

And she did.

Not that Grandpa had to do without home-made bakery goods entirely. Sometimes Grandma would say to my mother, "Margaret, next time you make light bread or rolls or doughnuts or whatever, bring your Papa some."

But, during the next several years, my mother discovered a bakery shop. She, too, got modern.

Grandma has been dead for 42 years now, but The Day she stopped making light bread and rolls and doughnuts is vivid in my mind. ◆

# Mama's Fruitcake

*By Ruth Kirkpatrick Townsend*

One of the nicest memories from my childhood is Mama's fruitcake and how it was made in the kitchen and aged in the parlor.

Mama used a recipe that had been handed down to her by her mother. It had been in the family for years. It had grape jelly in it, and chocolate, too, if you can imagine such a combination. Some of the instructions weren't very exact, and the recipe just said to put in spices

to taste. Mama finally wrote down the main ingredients pretty definitely, but she always just shook in the cinnamon and nutmeg and such. You'll find the recipe at the end so you can try it if you want to, and I hope you will want to.

When Mama got ready to make fruitcake, she always took down the big dishpan from where it hung on the wall of the entryway. Every time she would say, "We need something big and this is the best thing we have." Mama would wash the dishpan well and set it on the kitchen table.

My sister and I always got busy then, cutting up the dates and nuts and setting out the candied fruit such as citron, raisins and currants.

Mama used homemade butter. She put it in the dishpan and made sure it was good and soft. If it wasn't just right, she took a spoon and chopped at it until it suited her. Then she mixed in the brown sugar. After that came the beaten eggs and the soda dissolved in the hot water. Then the flour and the spices.

After all that was mixed in, my sister and I got to put in the fruits and nuts. We each got to take a turn, trying to stir the mixture, but usually we just weren't strong enough to do it the way Mama wanted. She held the dishpan up against her stomach and stirred vigorously. Then she stopped to grate a couple of squares of chocolate. The chocolate kind of fluffed up as she grated it so two squares were enough usually to fill 3 tablespoons.

After the chocolate, she put in the jelly. It was always homemade jelly. We loved to look at it and smelled of the ripe grapes we had picked under the late summer sun.

For baking, the batter was put in waxed paper-lined bread pans. Mama made sure the fire in the big cookstove had died down properly. Fruitcake had to cook slowly.

After the cakes came out of the oven, they were set aside to cool completely. Then Mama peeled off the waxed paper very carefully. After that, each loaf had to be wrapped in a fresh piece of waxed paper and finally covered entirely with a clean dish towel. Then all the cakes were packed in an old airtight metal bread box to mellow. The bread box stood on a table in the northwest corner of the cool, dark parlor.

When Christmastime finally arrived, Mama would go into the parlor to open the bread box. My sister and I would tag along. We loved the delicious smell of the fruits and nuts when she opened the lid. Mama let one of us carry the chosen cake out into the dining room.

With bated breath we watched Mama unwrap it. She took her sharpest knife and cut some thin, very thin, slices. Mama always said, "Fruitcake is rich, you know, and little girls can't have too much," so my sister and I would share a slice.

Papa got a big piece. He always said he married Mama so he could have her fruitcake every Christmas. We laughed at his little joke and then sat down to enjoy our piece of cake.

Modern fruitcakes are good, but for true Christmas joy, try making Mama's fruitcake for your family. There's nothing better to bring the joy of Christmas into your home. ◆

### Mama's Fruitcake

2 cups butter *or* margarine, softened
2½ cups brown sugar
7 beaten eggs
1 teaspoon baking soda dissolved in 2 tablespoons hot water
4 cups flour
½–1 teaspoon ground cinnamon
½–1 teaspoon ground nutmeg
Other spices to taste

1 pound raisins
1 pound currants
1 pound dates
½ pound citron
1 cup chopped nuts
2 cups candied fruits, or more to taste
3 tablespoons grated chocolate
½ cup grape jelly

Into softened butter, blend brown sugar, then eggs, then dissolved baking soda, blending thoroughly after each addition. Stir in flour and spices; mix well.

Stir in fruits and nuts, blending well. Mix in grated chocolate, blending thoroughly. Blend in jelly, mixing well.

Line greased bread pans with waxed paper; divide fruitcake batter among prepared pans. Bake in a 275- or 300-degree oven for 1 hour, or until done.

Set pans on rack to cool. When cool, carefully peel off waxed paper. Wrap each loaf in fresh waxed paper, and then in a clean dish towel or cheesecloth. Set aside in a cool, dark place for at least a week to allow fruitcakes to mellow.

# Mom's Grocery List

*By Helen Colwell Oakley*

Mom's grocery list was almost sacred. We lived miles from town. If Mom was out of anything or getting low on supplies from the grocery store, she jotted it down on the grocery list in a hurry, because if she forgot, we would have to do without until the next trip into town for groceries, and that could be several days.

Mom cooked for a houseful—Dad, the hired men, nine children and herself. Her grocery list would go all the way down one page and then resume on the back of the page. Flour and sugar were on the list often—in 100-pound bags, because Mom did lots of baking. Sometimes she would order 5 pounds of lard, but my city aunts were making cakes with Crisco and Spry and telling about the magical things it did for baking, so she would jot it down on the list occasionally. Crisco and Spry were supposed to make pies and cakes lighter and fluffier, among other things, but Mom didn't care much for newfangled ideas, saying that you couldn't teach an old dog new tricks. Anyway, her vanilla cake made with plain lard and topped with heavy cream was beyond compare—by far the best cake I have ever tasted.

In the winter, Mom bought large boxes of Mother's Oats. We ate this for breakfast most every morning, except when we had pancakes and fresh pork slices. Mom fixed up her own pancakes from scratch, with buttermilk, flour, baking soda and a little cornmeal. Cornmeal was always on the list as we loved Mom's johnnycake. She made a large pan of it, and it would be gone in a flash, it was that good.

I remember Argo starch for clothes and bottles of bluing on Mom's grocery lists. She called rolls of toilet paper "music rolls," and we always joked about this. Mom was always ordering spices—nutmeg, cloves, etc. She had so many cans of spices on her shelves that when I married, she filled small containers with each spice so I would have a full array for cooking.

Mom bought large wedges of sharp cheese, as Dad liked to eat cheese and crackers, and the family loved macaroni and cheese. She never failed to have peanut butter on her list—it was bought by the pound in those days and wrapped in a cardboard box. Mom put it in a jar, but it didn't stay moist and it wasn't easy to spread after a few days. Most every kid in the one-room school I attended brought peanut-butter sandwiches—we loved them, but the darn stuff stuck on the top of your mouth, and you had a rough time getting it loose. Peter Pan peanut butter was just coming out and, of course, Mom couldn't afford that because it was expensive and we used so much of it. What a delectable taste treat it was to sample some Peter Pan peanut butter at my city aunt's house!

Mom always had graham crackers and saltines on her list, buying large boxes of each. My children find it hard to believed that we ate a few grahams or saltines with a glass of milk and thought it was a good afternoon snack. My children want a cookie with their milk after school. We also sprinkled sugar on a slice of butter bread for a snack. What a kooky idea, my children think! But it was real popular when I was little, so there!

Fels Naptha soap, P&G and Ivory soap were on Mom's lists most every week. Mom didn't have soap powders or detergents—she shredded bars of P&G or Fels Naptha into a pot of boiling water, and when it was melted, she poured it into the Maytag washer.

Waxed paper came in sheets of pale green or white, but it came in such small quantities that we saved bread wrappers to wrap our school lunches. My sisters and I didn't like anyone to see our lunches wrapped in bread wrappers, though, and how the lunch boxes stunk! They seemed to have such a stale odor. We liked to carry our lunches in bags.

Sometimes Mom would have a new broom or scrub brush on the list. A good broom cost 98 cents. Yes, Mom did test her cakes with a broom straw.

Dried codfish was on Mom's list, also. She got it in wooden boxes and the top slid open. She parboiled it and then made a very tasty gravy to pour over boiled potatoes.

She bought 1-pound boxes of confectioners' sugar for frosting.

Oyster crackers were purchased in a good-size cardboard box. They lasted for only a week

or two and were great dunked in Mom's homemade soups.

Dried northern beans and limas were bought by the pound and came in a brown paper bag, to make Mom's sugar beans and baked limas. Mom also ordered macaroni and rice just about every grocery order—these were staples that were always kept on hand. Mom had cornstarch on most every grocery list; she used it to make delicious cornstarch puddings, and for thickening pies, gravies and sauces.

At holiday time, there were candied fruits and net bags of walnuts and mixed nuts. We always helped Mom crack the nuts so that they would be ready for the holiday treats. At Christmastime, at the top of the grocery list, there would always be tangerines and oranges to be tucked into the stockings on Christmas Eve. Corn for popping was on the list, too. We made popcorn balls and threaded popped corn with a needle and thread to hang on the Christmas tree—it was very decorative.

Eight O'Clock coffee from the A&P was on every list.

Sometimes, if we came upon Mom's grocery list as we dusted the desk, we couldn't resist jotting down "candy, peanuts, gum, bananas, dates and watermelon." If she could budget it in, we would get a candy or fruit treat every now and then.

Mom's large grocery orders kept the store clerk hopping. (How different it is today! You must do the running around to find the supplies yourself.) The back of our Buick would be brimming with kids, groceries and Mom and Dad as we started for home. Mom's groceries usually came to around $10. We had our own milk, butter, eggs, poultry, meat and fruits and vegetables.

Couldn't resist telling you about the pearl tapioca on Mom's list. She soaked it overnight and then cooked it until it was shiny pearls, and then made us a luscious tapioca pudding. The good old days have such pleasant memories! ◆

# Aunt Annie

*By Birdie L. Etchison*

Aunt Annie wasn't famous; she wasn't brilliant, nor was she beautiful. She was just Aunt Annie, a rawboned giant of a woman who was all tenderness one minute, stern and commanding the next. There wasn't a life she came in contact with that wasn't changed to some degree. She didn't have money, but an overdose of good old-fashioned wisdom more than made up for that.

I can see Aunt Annie now, bent over her enormous black wood stove, baking sour cream biscuits—the taste of which has never been duplicated—or whipping up a sponge cake out of a mere three eggs (some of them double-yolked, to be sure).

*She didn't have money, but an overdose of good old-fashioned wisdom more than made up for that.*

The old farmhouse where she had lived since her marriage in 1900 was big and roomy. How well I remember the walk-in pantry where rows of fruits and vegetables filled the wooden shelves. There was always plenty of food there. No trouble if extra guests dropped in; just open another jar of beans and tomatoes, whip up a second batch of biscuits and slice the roast beef a little thinner.

When supper was ready, a trip to the old washbasin was in order. Even now I can feel the water going down my arms and dripping off my elbows. After everyone had washed, Aunt Annie opened the door and gave the water a fast fling out into the yard.

There was a singing teakettle on the stove. Out of it came the water to wash up, water to wash the dishes after dinner, and another kettle filled with boiling water for the rinse. It was fun to pour the water from bowl to glass to cup, and then into the little pan that held the silverware.

The living room and dining room were filled with old cane-back rockers, each decorated with a different cover, none of which was purchased from the general store—heaven forbid!

Idleness was unheard of in Aunt Annie's day. When she sat in the evening by the kerosene lamp, the knitting needles were clicking, or the crochet hook went in and out. Watching the quick flash of needles could put me to sleep. Crocheted doilies graced end tables and the arms of the couch and overstuffed chairs.

I can still remember the creak of a spring gate. The path up to the front porch was not of hard concrete, but a dirt walk, packed down from years of use. The beloved porch ran the full length of the house, with a porch swing at one end. I can still hear the squeak it made when I sat in it and a cousin with longer legs made it swing back and forth, back and forth.

Walking through the orchard on a crisp fall day, listening to my feet crunching in the newly fallen leaves, was another treat, as was collecting the yellow banana apples to carry home in bushel baskets, and selecting the choicest pumpkins from the field.

Out back was the small wooden shed with its pungent smell of grain. Here the grain was stored for winter—enough to feed the chickens and rabbits.

Next came the smell of the barn, freshly mown hay and warm milk as it squirted into large, shiny buckets. The smell, the feel of a cow's flank against my forehead, the swishing of a tail. In the winter, we made hay houses in the barn. We'd remove a couple bales of hay, sit on the scratchy stuff, and chew on a piece of straw.

One of the best times was when the baby calves were born. The tiny newborn calves stood on wobbly legs, crying for their mamas, then finally found the good, sweet milk that nourished them.

Who can forget going after the cows at 5 p.m. each evening? It was a never-ending wonderment how those cows knew when to head for home.

Then there was the old well with its hand pump. Rather than lower a bucket into the well, we could crank the pump, and after three tries, sparkling water came gurgling out, filling the bucket to overbrimming seven cranks later.

I drove out past Aunt Annie's one day last spring. The weathered, gnarled apple trees still stood in the orchard, their white blossoms filling the air with sweetness, but the house no longer stands. In its place sits a low, modern structure. It's just another house now—the type you see dotting the landscape everywhere. The charm is gone.

Shiny-nosed, freckle-faced children play in the side yard. "Oh, what you are missing!" I long to call out to them. "Oh, what you have missed!" ◆

*"Oh, what you are missing!" I long to call out to them.*

### Antebellum Potato Pone

2 quarts grated, pared sweet potatoes
1 pint Jamaica molasses
1 pound dark brown sugar
½ pound butter
1 tablespoon ground ginger
1 teaspoon salt
1 teaspoon ground cloves
1 teaspoon ground cinnamon
1 teaspoon dried orange peel

Combine all ingredients thoroughly. Pour into a greased and floured 3-inch-deep pan and bake in a slow oven for 3 hours. Serve hot with a hard sauce seasoned with vanilla extract and grated nutmeg,

—*Mrs. Glenn (Ada) Sheets*

### Pumpkin Soup

Get a medium-size pumpkin. Peel and dice. Put into pot and add very little water. Cover and cook until tender. Mash the pumpkin. Add milk, as much as you like.

In the meantime, make some dumplings and drain them. Add dumplings to the pumpkin and milk. Add salt, pepper and butter to taste, or sugar instead of the salt, pepper and butter.

—*Mrs. Catherine Dutkiewicz Lee*

# Chapter 4

## Around The Kitchen

I learned to sing while doing the dishes. That may sound silly, but it's true. One of the chores my sister Donna and I had was to wash and dry the supper dishes. One day she washed while I dried; the next we alternated. There we would sing together: "Oh Mister Moon, Moon, bright and silv'ry Moon, won't you please shine down on me?" We traveled down by the old mill stream where I saw K-K-K-Katy, beautiful Katy, or dreamed of Jeannie with the light brown hair.

It's a lot easier to learn to sing looking out a small kitchen window knowing that your only audience is your dog out on the front porch. Thankfully, he didn't have much of an ear for music. The rest of our audience was probably laughing, but at least it was behind our backs. Since those days I have been in quite a few church choirs, barbership quartets and bands, but I don't think I have ever enjoyed singing more than with my little sister as we developed voices—and dishpan hands.

These stories, like that memory, brings smiles from around the kitchens of the Good Old Days.

—Ken Tate

# Homemade Ice Cream

*By Henry M. Flowers*

Nothing brings back more pleasant memories of one's youth than the mention of homemade ice cream. This delicacy has not been lost entirely, because many families still make their own ice cream, believing it to be a special treat. However, it surely cannot come up to Mother's recipe.

Each of the children in our family found a special reward in consuming two or three dishes of ice cream on those very special days near a small town in northern Ohio 60 years ago.

It usually took some urging to get Mother to agree to mix the ingredients for homemade ice cream. A 6-quart cylinder could not be frozen at a minute's notice; it took cooperation from several members of the family. A cake of ice was essential and could be hauled from town by us boys in our little wagon, or by Dad, if he happened to be making a trip in the buggy or wagon. Mother had to look ahead and save the milk and other ingredients. The shiny metal freezer cylinder and wooden stirring paddles had to be washed.

Mother would tell a couple of us boys to get the ice ready while she mixed the ingredients. It usually fell to my brother Frank and me to freeze the ice cream, and while we stabbed off pieces of ice with an ice pick, and put it in an old gunnysack to crush it with a board, Mother was putting together her ice cream recipe. She used nearly 5 quarts of fresh milk and added dissolved junket tablets, sugar, two raw eggs, a pinch of salt, a tablespoon of vanilla, and a full quart of pure cream. This done, Mother would place the stirring paddles into the cylinder and put the lid on, leaving the top of the paddle mechanism projecting through the hole.

We would no sooner be set up on the windmill platform with what we thought was enough crushed ice than Mother would come out, carefully carrying the rather heavy cylinder. "Now it's up to you boys," she would say as she carefully lowered the can into the wooden freezer keg, "and be careful you don't spill any." We engaged the turning mechanism to the top of the stirring paddles and clamped it down.

"OK, let's put in the ice," Frank said as Mother went back into the house. I started putting in the ice, using my hands as scoops. Brother started to turn the crank. As the ice built up around the metal cylinder, I put in a handful of salt occasionally to make it melt faster so it would take the heat out of the milk more quickly. Finally the ice covered the lid.

I relieved Frank at the crank which turned easily at this stage. The handle turned cogs to make the cylinder revolve slowly around the paddle apparatus inside, which in turn stirred the milk and exposed it to the cold sides of the can.

It was necessary to add ice and salt from time to time. Cold water began to run from a hole well toward the top of the wooden keg—it being there for that purpose—and we knew the ice was melting properly. Brother and I took turns at the crank and, after about 10 minutes, it began to turn a little harder. It was a few minutes more before the ice cream began to freeze enough so it made the crank turn much harder.

"It must be about ready now," I said as I took another turn, "but let's give it a couple minutes more just to be sure."

As the turns became harder and harder, I told my brother to go tell Mother the ice cream was done. She came out with a bowl and a large spoon. We unclamped the mechanism, lifted it off, and lifted the top of the cylinder out of the ice so Mother could remove the lid.

A glorious sight greeted our eyes! We were looking at the top of delicious-looking creamy ice cream.

"It's done," Mother said as she reached down and placed a thumb on the rim of the cylinder while she began to pull out the paddles. It came out slowly as the ice cream was cold and thick, but in a minute, Mother had the paddles out after scraping off some of the clinging ice cream with the spoon. She laid the paddles in the bowl and told me to get another spoon.

It was then that Frank and I had part of our reward for making the ice cream, because Mother had left a substantial amount of the creamy stuff on the blades. It was so good it disappeared quickly.

Mother had replaced the lid on the can, and we placed fresh ice and salt over it after draining out most of the water. Then we draped the wet gunnysack over the freezer and carried it to the shade of the porch where it would remain until Mother was ready to serve the ice cream.

None of us had to be reminded to save room for the ice cream while we ate dinner. If we had had our way, we would have eaten nothing but ice cream.

The time finally came for Mother to scoop out heaping dishes of ice cream. These gone, most of us raided the freezer for second helpings. A few of us would return later in the day for yet another dish until, by evening, the 6-quart freezer was empty.

Yes indeed, homemade ice cream remains one of the most vivid and happy memories of our childhood years! ◆

# A Chilling Tale

*By Louise Schasre*

Whenever I open my refrigerator door or remove a package from the freezer, I cannot help thinking about the days when we had to find other ways to keep food cold. I grew up in an era when electric refrigerators were taking the place of iceboxes, but we could not afford either device. Some of the rich people we knew, such as my father's employer, enjoyed chilled orange juice for breakfast in July. We considered ourselves fortunate to obtain free ice suckers on hot summer days.

A horse-drawn wagon with the word "ICE" painted in chilly blue letters on its wooden side panels was a common sight on our street. Huge cakes of ice were piled inside the wagon. The wagon's floorboards were assembled with wide cracks between to allow the melting ice to drip through, and the ice was covered with sawdust as insulation against the heat. The iceman would drag a big chunk of ice to the rear of the wagon and hit it where he wanted it to separate. Then he would chop along the line, scattering icy fragments in all directions. We gathered the ice chips and tied them inside clean handkerchiefs, making refreshing ice suckers to quench our thirst

*I grew up when electric refrigerators were taking the place of iceboxes, but we could not afford either device.*

AMERICA'S MOST FAMOUS DESSERT

JELL-O

A MIXTURE
DELICATE DELIGHTFUL DAINTY

LEMON
PURE FRUIT FLAVOR

VEGETABLE COLOR

THE GENESEE PURE FOOD CO., LE ROY

and cool us off. We watched the iceman hoist the ice onto his rubber-sheeted back with tongs and carry it into the customer's house.

We were never one of the customers who placed one of those little cardboard signs in the front window to inform the iceman how many pounds of ice we wanted. Our family had to rely on other means to chill food. My grandmother had a root cellar underground that kept bottles of milk sweet for days, or butter solid, or meat fresh. But it was never cold enough to freeze ice cream during the hottest months when we longed for that refreshment. It kept oranges cold in winter, when Grandma could afford to buy oranges—usually at Christmastime and Easter. And it chilled her home-canned strawberries nicely, so they slid down a sore throat soothingly when we kids caught a cold or, as it was known in those days, the "grippe."

Our own little house had no root cellar, but there was a stairway leading to an unheated attic which became our icebox. The attic was insulated poorly, so it became quite cold in winter, just as it was unbearably hot in summer. The door leading to the attic was in our kitchen, which made it convenient as a storage area. The kitchen was the warmest room in the house during our cold Buffalo winters, especially while meals were baking in the oven of our gas stove. I can recall the delicious aroma of meat loaf, baked potatoes and squash as I sat beside the stove on a tall metal stool, reading a book from the library. The book was propped against the oven, and its warmed pages comforted my fingers.

*A horse-drawn wagon with the word "ICE" painted in chilly blue letters on its wooden side panels was a common sight on our street. We were never one of those who placed one of those little cardboard signs in the front window to inform the iceman how many pounds of ice we wanted. We relied on other means to chill food.*

When we needed something from our "icebox," I would set the book aside and open the attic door. Frigid air would blast my flushed cheeks for a moment, but it was never unpleasant, for with it came the good smells of all the foods that were stored on the stairs—a large white kettle of ham and cabbage; a crock of sauerkraut; a china dish with a chunk of cheese; bananas; a glass bowl with some leftover boiled onions, covered with a flowered saucer to keep out the dust. When we had company for Sunday dinner, there would be pretty glass dishes of bright red Jell-O topped with whipped cream.

Making the Jell-O was a problem. The stairway was chilly enough to keep the gelatin solid, but not quite cold enough to set it quickly when we had unexpected company. We had no ice cubes to hasten the process, so we usually carried a glass bowl of the liquid Jell-O out onto the front porch and set it in a few inches of snow. That worked well, until one wintry evening when I caught a neighborhood cat sampling the contents of the bowl.

After that we used the milk box beside our back door. It was too shallow to accommodate a round bowl, so we had to leave the outside door open when making Jell-O. My mother considered this an open invitation to neighborhood boys who were known to raid people's milk boxes from time to time. In extremely cold weather, the milk in the tall bottles would freeze. The top part would force its way out the top of the bottle, covered only by a small round cardboard cap. Since milk in those days was not homogenized, the part at the top was pure cream. This was a great temptation to roving boys who enjoyed biting off the inch or two of frozen cream, then replacing the cardboard cap as if nothing had happened. The only evidence we had of their mischief was a thawed bottle of milk that was not quite filled to the top.

Whenever I see little boys trying to snatch something for nothing out of a supermarket bulk food container, I recall how much fun it was for the kids to snitch the iced milk, and I try to remember that kids will be kids, no matter the era in which they live. I suspect the children of the 2000s will look back at the automatic freezers, ice crushers and food chillers of today and say, "How old-fashioned!"

But I'm also certain that they will think of the fun they had licking their Popsicles, instant drinks and ices of all kinds and say, "The 1990s were sure the good old days!" ◆

### Tapioca Jell-O

4 tablespoons pearl tapioca
2 quarts boiling water
2 boxes strawberry Jell-O
1 cup sugar
½ cup heavy cream, whipped

Stir pearl tapioca into boiling water. Remove pan from heat; stir in Jell-O and sugar and stir very well, until both are completely dissolved. Let cool, then refrigerate until partially thickened. Stir in whipped cream and chill until firm.

—*Mrs. Ray S. Kinsinger*

# A New Tablecloth

*By Goldie Counts*

I have many pleasant childhood memories. I guess most folks do. More and more, I notice unpleasant memories have faded and lost whatever crushing effect they had at the time. On the other hand, the pleasant memories intensify, becoming more beautiful with the embroidery of nostalgia.

One such memory is of Mama getting a new oilcloth covering for the kitchen table. We did not have a dining room, so the big kitchen table was our dining table. As I remember it, the oilcloth of that day did not wear nearly as well as today's vinyl tablecloths.

How a new covering brightened up the kitchen! Sometimes it was covered with yellow daisies; sometimes, bright red cabbage roses! Always, it was beautiful—and the new smell was beautiful, too.

Nothing was ever wasted in those days, so the old tablecloth was trimmed to remove the worn corners, and became a new cover for the little table in the corner, on which the pails of drinking water sat. I'm sure the old cover from the little table found some use somewhere, too. Today, when my spirits need a boost, I close my eyes and open my memory box. The table is set with mismatched dishes, but it is beautiful! The kitchen is warm, bright and noisy, and everyone's spirits are lifted by the new tablecloth. ◆

# Mom's Old Table

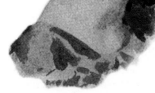

*By Velma Ludd*

I have often thought of the secrets that old table could tell if it could only talk. It was almost like a living, breathing member of the family. I didn't know whether to call it a her or an it. Through the years it stood proudly in the big dining room, on its pedestal-style legs. The dining room was like our family rooms of today—big, with comfortable chairs, and the place where so much of our big family's activity took place. Most everyone remembers the big, round, oak tables, only ours was   always oblong to accommodate our large family.

On school evenings many of us were grouped around the table, studying our lessons. That table must have been content, knowing we were gaining a little knowledge.

On other nights, a big circle of kids gathered there, crunching popcorn—or, if it was summer, consuming  melons, dripping juice and making the table weepy.

Many games were played around the table. There were kibosh, old maid, hearts, crazy eights and many others. Laughter and giggles could be heard, and probably some extra giggles when one thought he was getting away with a little cheating.

A big reading lamp hung over the table and we did our reading there with a book plunked down in front of us. We read everything—picture

books, fairy tales, *The Bobbsey Twins* and even a little Shakespeare.

Sometimes that table looked all dressed up, in its long, white tablecloth and the Sunday-best china. Company was coming!

Other times the table was dressed in its everyday wear—a checked or white oilcloth. After each meal, her skirts were lifted daintily while her corners were washed. She always looked dignified, even in her everyday garb.

Sometimes we sat around her and picked out nuts that had been cracked on an old flatiron. Many tummies were filled before enough were collected for the cake, cookies or nut bread.

For a quick ironing board, we covered one end of the old table with an old blanket. To

this day there are iron marks on the top of Mom's table.

We worked on many crafts there: coloring, painting, cornhusk dolls, paper roses, valentines, apple heads, Easter eggs, clothespin dolls and Christmas ornaments, to name a few.

When there was sewing to be done, a stretched-out table was the ideal place to cut a pattern, and many were cut out for our large group. I remember an aunt making a prom dress, and a few years later, a wedding dress was cut out for the same girl. Then Mom's table was all dressed up in her own long white gown for the wedding reception.

Then there was threshing time; you have heard of "threshers' dinners." That table really groaned under the load of food, but I am sure the table also grinned to see the food being poked into those happy faces.

There were the big turkeys it held at Thanksgiving, and the fat, roasted chickens at Christmastime, along with the dressing, cranberries, cakes and pies.

When friends came to call, we had coffee or lemonade, depending on the time of year. How much one can enjoy just sitting around a comfortable table, talking!

One of the grandchildren couldn't understand why there were salt and pepper, cream and sugar, and butter at both ends of the table. She didn't realize the extra leaves that had to be added to accommodate company. It would have wasted a lot of time, passing the essentials such a long way around.

Kids of all sizes sat around that table, and each had his own place at mealtime. Every time there was a new baby, the seating arrangement changed. The youngest child sat between Mother and Father. When it came time for another child to eat at the table, the next youngest moved.

When I think of all the abuse those legs must have suffered from our kicking feet, I wonder, Old Table, why didn't you just kick back, and not just grin and bear it?

Saturday was known as "spit-and-polish" day, when everything got cleaned and scrubbed—including Mom's table. I am sure it felt good to have her legs washed and polished at the end of the week.

Little ones played under the table. Many a time it served as a playhouse, and the kids' conversations were always interesting. Old Table, did they sometimes tickle your funny bone?

There were times when that table saw one of us get a thunk on the head for not minding our manners.

I remember when the table got broken. How it must have laughed to know how we depended on it. If the old table could, I think it would have winked when it knew how much we needed it. What a catastrophe to be without a table!

And the birthday cakes that old table held— birthday parties must have been invented to give special joy in a child's life. The summer birthday parties always had cake and lemonade, candy and peanuts, but the winter ones included ice cream. Those were the times we got out the big ice cream freezer and all took turns turning the crank. How happy the table must have been when there was a kids' party, with all its laughter, fun and games.

> *When friends came to call, we had coffee or lemonade, depending on the time of year. How much one can enjoy just sitting around a comfortable table, talking!*

Even boyfriends were entertained around the piece of old oak, and I am sure there was much hand-holding. Did you close your eyes, Old Table, or did you peek? You must have leaped with joy when you saw a ring slipped on a finger.

What a happy harvest of memories we reaped from that old table through the years!

The smaller children wrote letters to Santa Claus around this table. Then their letters were thrown into the stove and burned so Santa Claus could read the smoke at the North Pole. The youngsters looked in the stove's warming oven for his answers to their letters. The older children enjoyed seeing how thrilled the younger ones were about Santa Claus, and never told the secret, so the youngsters enjoyed the mystery for many years.

When I think of that old table, I think of the times it warmed a heart, welcomed friend and stranger, entertained a boyfriend, toasted a bride, fed the hungry, surprised a child, and just made happy times for everyone.

Old Table, how could we have gotten along without you? There were times when I would have loved to have reached out and hugged that old table for the joy and comfort it gave us.

And where is Mom's old table today? It is in the home of a granddaughter, finding out secrets from three children—and starting a whole new life. ◆

# Learning to Do the Dishes

*By Helen Colwell Oakley*

Learning to do the dishes was a very important part of a little girl's life when I was growing up in the late '20s. Now, with automatic dishwashers, most little girls will probably miss the fun and satisfaction which come from learning to do the dishes.

As a girl grew older, when there were parties, shopping trips and boyfriends, washing and drying the dishes was a chore to be avoided, if possible. But for a little girl, it was a most enjoyable experience. When I was 3 or 4, my Grandmother Coy allowed me to help clear the table. I collected the soiled silver from all around the large dining-room table until I had made the complete circle.

"Tis best to keep the forks, knives and spoons all heading one way," said Grandmother Coy. If I accidentally dropped one on the floor, she would say, "Oops! We're about to have a visitor. Let me see who's coming." A fork meant a lady visitor. A knife meant a gentleman was coming to call, and a teaspoon would bring a child to Grandma's for a visit. How exciting it was to watch for a visitor—and sometimes we would have one!

Grandma Coy used a large aluminum dishpan in the sink for washing the dishes and another large pan alongside for scalding them. Before we sat down to eat, the large teakettle with a black shiny handle was filled with water to scald the dishes, after they were washed in hot sudsy water. Ivory soap and P&G were popular for dishwashing in those days. Fels-Naptha soap was best for cutting the grease, my mom thought, but it was hard on the hands. There were no rubber gloves or gentle detergents to help milady in the dishpan.

A pretty bottle of hand lotion sat on most every windowsill above the sink. The ladies and big girls rubbed the lotion into their hands after doing the dishes. Some of the lotions were homemade or bought from someone in the neighborhood who made up a large batch and bottled it. It was a delicate pink and smelled like roses—what a heavenly fragrance!

When I was a little older, I helped to scrape the soiled dishes and stack them. But I wasn't allowed to carry the large stacks of dishes into the kitchen—Gram always did this chore. I took the scraps out to the back porch for Gram's dog and cats. They always howled and meowed after meals so that we would not forget to feed them. Gram was very good to them, so they did not have to wait long.

*Learning to do the dishes was a very important part of a little girl's life when I was growing up in the late '20s.*

After the tablecloth was shaken out over the porch railing, it was returned to the table for the next meal, unless it was soiled. (Gram always liked a fresh, white tablecloth on the dining-room table and a pretty flowered oilcloth for the kitchen table.) Then the carpet sweeper was brought out to clean up the crumbs under the table. "Part of doing dishes is tidying up the dining room and kitchen and being sure everything is left as clean as it was before the meal was prepared," advised Grandmother Coy.

The glassware was washed first, when the water was cleanest. This helped make it sparkle and shine. The silver came next. I didn't like the forks; they were too sharp, and sometimes when the water was sudsy, I couldn't see the tines until I was pricked. The dinner plates were quite heavy for a little girl, but I enjoyed scrubbing them with the dishcloth until they were shiny and clean. I liked to do the cups and saucers best of all. I spent quite a few minutes pouring the sudsy water back and forth into the cups and having a wonderful time, until one slipped from my little fingers. Once I broke the handle off a teacup. I felt very bad that Gram couldn't fix it. She didn't scold, but I knew that I should be extra careful when I was washing the teacups.

I didn't do the pot and pans until I was more grown-up, around 11 or so. I never liked this part of doing the dishes too well because the water would get greasy, and it was hard to work up suds. Besides, the food

would stick and take lots of scrubbing and scraping to come clean. We used Old Dutch Cleanser to scour the pots and pans and to clean and polish the sink.

After the dishes were rinsed and scalded, they were set carefully on the drain board of the sink unless someone was drying as they were washed. When entertaining at dinner, part of the evening or afternoon was spent, most enjoyably, helping to do the dishes. Secrets were divulged, juicy bits of gossip exchanged, recipes given and advice sought and given over a sinkful of dishes. The job always seemed lighter with all the extra hands, though. There was most always laughing and joviality, and sometimes a few tears.

My sisters and I would draw straws or take a number out of a hat to see which one would wash or dry the dishes, and when the cousins came, we got them involved so we would have extra help. Drying the dishes was more popular than washing. No one liked to do the pots and pans.

One time when my mother was called away in an emergency, my sister Fran, who was about 10, did the dishes all by herself and had everything spic-and-span by the time Mom returned.

Later Mom discovered that Fran had given each of our two dogs and each several cats a bowl, serving dish, frying pan or saucepan to "clean up." At the time, Mom was more than a little upset, but she laughed as she related the story through the years.

Today I, too, have a dishwasher, but I often do the dishes by hand, just to bring back the memories of yesteryear.

A most pleasant part of doing the dishes was choosing a pretty tea towel or dish towel from the towel drawer. Some were handmade, adorned with crocheting and sometimes an edge of lace that was also hand-crocheted.

The ladies were very proud of their "good" tea towels and dish towels, and a gift of tea towels or dish towels was always welcome. I always took special delight in drying the dishes with a colorful towel, and I still do.

I miss the long housedresses and large aprons the ladies used to wear when I was a little girl. And the kitchens were so cozy, with a singing teakettle on the wood-burning stove, a filled woodbox, a rocking chair with a kitten curled up in a ball, and a batch of bread ready to be popped into the oven. ◆

# Stoves I Have Known

*By Lois Waterworth*

The delivery truck from the local appliance store pulls into the driveway. Eagerly, the young homemaker rushes out to greet the deliveryman as he opens the big doors and pulls out a large square box with the words "Range—This side up." Her new stove has arrived and she is delighted. It may be a large gas or electric, and will be available in a rainbow of colors—copper, maybe, or avocado or sunshine yellow or poppy. Regardless of its make or color, you may be assured of one thing: It will do just about anything in the world you would wish a stove to do. It is automatic to the last degree, and anyone with the ability to push buttons may become a connoisseur overnight.

Alas, it was not always so.

**The young homemaker's new stove has arrived and she is delighted.**

As a bride in 1905, my mother came to a new house filled with furniture in a small town in Northwest Missouri. Not the least of her treasures was a coal-black, cast-iron and nickel-plate wonder in her kitchen, her wood-burning range. How proud she was of the curlicues and scrollwork on the oven door. The intricate designs were repeated on the front of the reservoir and the firebox.

It stood on four elegantly sculpted legs. Towering above was the roomy warming closet. At the right end was a 4-gallon reservoir of galvanized iron so that there was no worry about rust. It gave her the great luxury of always having hot water handy for washing dishes, milk buckets or little boys' faces.

Each of the four or six holes on the stove's surface was fitted with a tight lid. One of these lids was made of three nesting circles which fit within one another, thus accommodating very small pans if one wished to cook over the open flame. A hole in each lid accommodated a convenient lid-lifter. If the lid-lifter was lost or broken, a replacement could be purchased at the hardware store for 3 cents.

The roomy oven could hold several pans of light bread or five or six pies all at once. It could happily accommodate a big, fat hen *and* a large pan of corn-bread dressing. Oh, there was no end of things that could come out of that oven! Of course, there was no temperature regulator, but one soon learned to get a good fire going, refuel it regularly, open the door and insert one's right hand to tell how hot it might be.

If there was anything a housewife needed, it was a good, dependable oven. However, it had other purposes than just baking food. When Father came in from the barn, half-frozen from

**Woodburning Stove**

doing chores on a sub-zero morning, how welcome was the warmth from the open oven door—providing, of course, that Mother had already removed the big flat pan of breakfast biscuits to the warming closet. On some wintry morning, Father might be carrying a chilled newborn lamb. Mother wrapped it in an old piece of blanket and laid it on the oven door until it was thawed out enough to return it to its worried mother.

The oven door was also a handy drying rack for wet shoes, socks and mittens. On rainy days or in cold weather, the wooden clothes rack was set in front of the oven and the clothes were hung a few at a time to dry. The room would be steamy-damp and the windows covered with fog, which by the way, made a great drawing board for the fingers of little children kept indoors by the weather.

When Saturday night finally rolled around, the galvanized washtub was carried from the smokehouse and installed in front of the oven door for the comfort and convenience of all.

The oven was a great source of comfort in the wintertime but, oh, the summertime! That was a different story. Regardless of the soaring temperature, the stove must be fired up every day. Mother must stand over it for long hours, not only to cook for her own family, but to cook for hands when it was haying time, or if there should be a houseful of company, or maybe a funeral, when everyone would come and stay for days.

Also, out in Mother's back yard was a prolific garden, and since everything matured in the hottest weather, and not one vegetable, green, yellow or red, was allowed to go to waste, the range was kept going full blast. Apple, peach and cherry trees also were bent low with abundant fruit, and it must all be carefully preserved. Jars and lids must be carefully scalded, the vegetables blanched in boiling water. After the jars were filled, they were placed in the wash boiler which contained enough boiling water to cover, and cooked for however long was necessary to meet Mother's requirements. The food must not spoil during the long months ahead, as the lives of her family depended on it.

Speaking of the wash boiler, it had its day of glory once a week, usually Monday morning. The washtubs must be brought out; the water must be heated in the boiler and then emptied into the tubs. Then the boiler was filled and Mother added lye to break the water. When the resulting scum was skimmed off, the water was then soft as rainwater. White clothes were all scrubbed on the washboard with her beautiful, white, homemade soap, and then were rinsed and placed in the boiler to simmer until their snowy whiteness hurt your eyes when they were hung in the sun.

Our boiler served an unusual purpose once. My brother was just a little lad and was suffering from a bad earache and high fever, resulting in a convulsion. Fortunately, Mother had just put the boiler on and the water was just comfortably warm, so she just picked up the baby, sat him down in the warm water and put a cold cloth on his head. That ended that convulsion.

One thing about Mother: She was always equal to the situation. All her babies were born at home in the big bed in the front bedroom. As soon as the new baby arrived, Rosie, the lady who always "stayed" with us during these times, wrapped the little mite in a blanket and carried it to the kitchen. There, before a roaring fire and open oven door, the little one was bathed and dressed before being carried back to Mother.

Oh, the old stove could have told many interesting stories if it could have talked, and it had a great and glorious day. But as with all things, its glory passed and the day finally came when it had to yield to progress and be replaced by a more modern invention.

Why this invention didn't blow us all to kingdom come I'll never know, but Dad proudly replaced the old range with a slightly used but very efficient gasoline stove. It had four burners on one end and a high oven on the other. A tank of gasoline was attached to the end next to the burners. The burners consisted of a circular trench through which the gasoline flowed.

Everyone knows you don't light gasoline with a match, and the stove was accompanied by a metal wand about 8 inches long. This wand was inserted in some of the gasoline in the trench, a match was struck and put to the gasoline on the wand, and the wand was reinserted in the trench, safely lighting the burner. Anyway, I guess it was safe.

Finally it was replaced by a real winner. Dad always loved to give Mother the best if he could, and it was with real pride that he brought home her beautiful new Perfection kerosene range. Oh, that was a big day at our house!

It was a soft cream color with green trim. There were four burners and a large oven. Each burner had a wick, much like a lamp wick, encased in a metal cylinder with an isinglass window. One tipped this cylinder back to light the wick, then lowered it again and the mellow glow came through the isinglass. The heat was controlled by raising or lowering the wick accordingly. This stove was very easy to use and produced excellent results. Its only disadvantage was that the glass tank on the side must be filled from a barrel outside the back door and it sometimes went dry right when you had a cake in the oven. We learned to check the tank before we started baking.

I have treasured memories of coming home to the smells of homemade bread and cinnamon

**Kerosene Stove**

rolls that the oven had produced, along with Mother's skill. And all this without the aid of a controlled oven or an automatic timer.

They say the kitchen is the heart of the home, and it's certain that the stove is the heart of the kitchen. ◆

### Bosom Bread

2 cups brown sugar
1 egg
1 cup heavy molasses
1 teaspoon ground ginger
Small amounts of ground allspice and ground cloves (optional)
2 teaspoons baking soda dissolved in 2 cups sour milk
Approximately 4 cups flour, depending on kind of molasses used

*Legend goes that the fellows loading cotton in Mississippi had no chance to stop to eat, so each carried a chunk of "bosom bread" in his shirt, grabbing a mouthful as he ran to and from the ships on the Mississippi River.*

*This recipe was brought from Mississippi by my aunt about 70 years ago. This gingerbread is very dark and heavy, but delicious, and it stays moist for a long time.*

—*Mrs. William S. Burrows*

# Whatever Happened to Mama's Silverware?

*By Joseph S. Hufhan*

In 1909, something happened to Mama's silverware that remained a mystery until 1910 rolled around.

In the spring of 1909 I was faced with a problem. Papa had moved our family to New Berlin, into the only available house—the A.C.L. section house a quarter of a mile outside the village.

I was 7 years old and I'd never seen a train in Shackletown, where I was born. But our new home was built on railroad property, and the porch was jammed up to the railroad ditch. I got my first thrill the first day we were moved in when I saw a great, black, breathing monster coming down the railroad from the direction of the port city of Wilmington. It passed so close to the house that I was sure I could have held onto the porch railing, swung out and touched it with my hand. It shook the house as it passed, and roared on into the village.

The next thrill came when larks from the savannah came sailing in to perch in Mr. Bob Applewhite's old field across the track to feed. Some perched in pines, turned their yellow breasts to the sun, and whistled some of the most beautiful, clearest notes I have ever heard.

My sister Ruth was four years older than I was, and she had an imagination more vivid than mine. There were no little boys around for me to play with, but Ruth would play with me sporadically—if I'd play dolls.

When the sun was sinking low, the larks flew up and headed for the savannah, and I felt homesick for Shackletown. Ruth noticed. She said, "Joe don't feel too bad. It will be dark by the time we finish supper. Then you and I will sit on the front porch and watch for the Maco ghost light."

"What is that?" I wanted to know. I had looked down 4 miles of track toward the flag stop called Maco, and had seen nothing but pines and pines and more pines on both sides of the right-of-way.

"It's the lantern light of a loyal railroad flagman who got killed at the Hood Creek trestle long before we were born. It comes bobbing up the track every night from the trestle to the Maco crossing," Ruth said.

We had no rural lights in New Berlin in those days; we ate supper by lamplight. Then Ruth and I took seats on the front porch. Papa had opened a market up in the heart of the village and he came home late. Ruth and I told him we had seen something way down the railroad.

Papa said, "No, that's not the ghost light. That's the switch light up at the flag stop."

The next thing to break through my blues was a tramp. Seated on the porch, I could see him way down the railroad. In those days not even a dirt road led past the section house to Maco. Now Highway 74–76 runs by and Highway 87 branches off beside where the section house stood. Tramps came by frequently, and they'd ask for water or a handout of food. I liked them to stop and tell us of faraway places.

This particular tramp, though, happened to be a peddler. When he stopped for water and a short rest, he sold Mama a set of silverware: knives, forks and spoons. Mama stored them away in a large cigar box. They were to be used when we had distinguished company such as a preacher, or at such a time as we wanted to put on the dog.

One rainy day I was plundering around in the house and found the box of silverware. I made a mental note of where it was. A few days later, my brother Dempsey and a Shackletown buddy, Rudolph Bodeaux, walked way down the track toward Maco. After awhile they came back running.

"Three bears came out on the railroad almost right at us!" they said. I made a mental note of that, too.

That night the talk was about a thoroughfare just below the section house which bears used to travel back and forth between the great green

swamp and the Cape Fear River lowlands, eating acorns along Lynscomb Branch.

At first I was almost too scared to stick my head out, but that was beginning to wear off when Mama got scared and scared the daylights out of Ruth and me.

That day Ruth was in a playing notion. She said, "Joe, let's go to the Spruce Pine Hill and play dolls. You have been wishing that Exie and Ruby would die, and we'll let one die."

"And let me bury her?" I answered. "All right, let's go."

Ruth got Exie and Ruby, both little girl dolls about 5 inches long. I didn't mean to play dolls. Spruce Pine Hill was about 70 yards along the railroad right-of-way, the cart road leading under the pine.

While Ruth was playing that Exie was sick and Ruby was tending to her, I sat in the sand burying one foot after the other, making toad-frog houses. I tired of that, so I said, "Ruth, isn't Exie dead yet?"

"Not quite," she answered, walling her big,

blue eyes at me. "I think, though, by the time you can dig a grave, she'll be gone. She's got no pulse and she's hardly breathing. Ruby has begun crying. That's a good sign."

I tore out for the house to get a spoon to dig the grave. I found the kitchen locked, so I crept into the house past where Mama was trying out her new Silver Star sewing machine, and slipped out with her whole box of silverware.

I went running up the road to Ruth. "Is Exie dead yet?" I asked.

"No, she has rallied just a little, but go ahead; be digging the grave."

The sand was mellow, yellow dirt. Digging was easy. I kept right on digging until I had an oblong grave about a foot deep.

I quit inquiring about Exie. I was cutting the grave to fit that box. Then I let the box of silverware down into the grave and covered it, making a little mound above it. I meant to dig it up as soon as Exie died and bury her, but it was at this point that we heard a call from the house.

The kitchen to the section house was separated from the house by a covered passageway. Mama stood on the passageway, beckoning. She called, "You children hurry to the house! There's a bear coming down the railroad from Maco!"

All the terror about bears Dempsey and Rudolph had stirred up in me came back and I outran Ruth to the house. No other member of our family was there. Mama pointed. Sure enough, about 200 yards away, we saw a black thing at the railroad bed.

"You children get into the house and keep perfectly quiet," Mama said. "I've thumb-bolted the front door, closed and locked the blinds. I'll lock this one, and the room door. We will stand at the window and peek through the blinds and see if he passes. If he tries to break it, I don't know what we'll do."

I rushed to the window immediately. Presently I saw a tall, black, shaggy thing pop into view. Ruth said, "Mama, it's a dog! He has a collar and a badge."

Mama was peeking between the blinds at the next window. She said, "Well, he might have been more fierce at you children than a bear. Don't go back to that hill today." And we didn't.

*In 1909, something happened to Mama's silverware that remained a mystery until 1910 rolled around.*

I'd been scared so bad I'd completely forgotten Mama's box of silverware. When Thanksgiving came, we had company and Mama wanted to put her silverware on the table, but no soap. Nobody could find the cigar box. I was questioned, but honestly, I didn't remember getting the box.

It wasn't until the next summer that Ruth took another doll-playing notion. She and Violet Manning, a neighborhood girl, carried Exie and Ruby to the Spruce Pine Hill to play, and I went along with the ash spoon we used in the kitchen. It so happened that I sat down to dig where I had dug a year before. I was digging away when I unearthed the cigar box. It was puffed up from getting wet many times.

"Ruth!" I exclaimed. "Here's Mama's silverware!" I opened the box and lo, Mama's "silverware" was coated with rust!

If that peddler ever passed that way again, it must have been on a train, for he must have had a premonition that Mama was just waiting to "crawl his kitchen" for cheating her so. ◆

# The Dinner Bell

*By Ruby Flatt*

Most farm homes had a dinner bell when I grew up in the Tennessee hills many years ago. When the housewife got the noon meal ready (we called it dinner), she would ring the bell for the field hands to come to the house and eat.

Our bell was just outside our kitchen door, mounted on a tall post. Mama pulled a rope attached to the bell to ring it. She said, "You children don't ring the bell long and loud enough." She could make the bell peal out its message of good things to eat waiting on the table. She rang the bell like there was an art to it; the strokes were loud and clear.

When I was helping in the field, I watched for the noonday sun to climb high in the sky. Then I shoved my sunbonnet back and listened for the bell to peal its sweet music. Even though I was exhausted from working in the scorching sun, the thought of a new blackberry cobbler with butter waiting for me on the table made me pick up my weary feet and step lively. It was easy to run down the steep hill.

I sometimes wondered if the tired work mules noticed the ringing of the bell, for then they could rest awhile too; their harness removed, they could eat, and drink cold water from the watering trough at the spring.

The bell was also used to announce an emergency. If the house or barn caught fire or someone had an accident, the bell was rung for help. The field hands came running, leaving the work mules standing in their tracks.

Mama feared the bell would be rung accidentally someday, and she said, "That could cause a real commotion." She had warned us children about ringing the bell.

Then it happened! Our cousins were visiting us from Nashville. The small boy rang the bell even though he had been told not to. It was midafternoon on a sweltering summer day. The menfolk were working in the field high on a hillside. When they heard the bell, they bolted for the house, holding onto their straw hats and

running those corn rows as if they weren't there. Of course, the menfolk were glad nothing was wrong, but they were riled and chewed more than their sweet tobacco.

The work mules left in the field ran away. The small boy from Nashville got some "peach-tree tea." His mother acted as if he had committed the unpardonable sin. He probably thought he had, for he gave up bell ringing for the rest of his life.

If I had one of those bells in my yard today, it would be a conversation piece. In fact, it probably would be thought a work of art! ◆

---

### When Grandma Rang the Dinner Bell

From the "south forty" over yonder,
You don't have to ponder
On the mighty clang and swell,
When Grandma rang the dinner bell!

Running in from the far-off places,
Fields of grain and open spaces,
Came young and old, who knew so well,
When Grandma rang the dinner bell!

It stood just out the kitchen door,
So she had but to cross the floor,
And open up the door a spell,
To run and ring the dinner bell.

When you're tired (and hungry, too),
Dinner means a lot to you,
With empty stomach and lunch pail,
You'll hear it ring without much fail.

I'm so accustomed to its call,
In summer, spring, winter, fall,
My hunger pains down in the dell—
Hear Grandma ring the dinner bell!

—*Nancy Halstenberg*

# My Cast Iron Skillet

*By Winifred M. Crowley*

The mod generation of kitchenware has everything from fondue pots to frying pans in dazzling arrays of colors. Lightweight, electric and easy-living utensils come in every size and shape that are lovely to look at and a delight to use. But on my kitchen shelf is a pan that surpasses them all—my cast-iron skillet. Old, discolored and work-worn, it plops like a dowdy grandmother among the new, style-conscious members of today's "pot-and-pan" set.

*In my early years of housekeeping I was unimpressed with this lackluster piece of equipment. It didn't fit my dreams of a bright and modern kitchen.*

In my early years of housekeeping I was unimpressed with this lackluster piece of equipment. It didn't fit my dreams of a bright and modern kitchen. The matronly lady who brought it as a gift to my bridal shower assured me that "what it lacked in beauty, it would make up in efficiency," but I really didn't believe her. It wasn't long, however, before I found that she was right. My more attractive utensils were soon bent out of shape, handleless, or so badly burned that they had to be thrown away. I began to reach more often for the pan that gave me no trouble, and that trustworthy skillet has seldom had a day of rest since.

I admit its battered, inelegant appearance can't compare with today's colorful cookery, but they can't match this skillet's versatility. For instance, it can simmer, stew, sauté, braise, brown, bake, roast, fry and fricassee, and it works equally well on the range surface or in the oven. It has served family-size meat pies, baked cakes, fried chickens, Swiss steaks, roasted ducks and warmed up leftovers, not to mention the 6 million hamburgers it has grilled.

Give Dad my iron skillet and a pancake turner and he becomes an instant chef, impressing his offspring with his ability to turn out golden French toast or scrambled eggs. Actually, the credit belongs to that wonderful pan, but I haven't had the heart to tell him. The dog, too, would dearly love to claim it for his own and I must admit the idea is tempting. What stray could heft a dish of this size and weight and pack it off?

Our family, like most Americans today, spends a good deal of time out-of-doors, but whether it's a backyard barbecue or a camping trip,

### Mother had an iron skillet, too.

my skillet becomes involved. Since it doesn't chip, scratch, break, bend or melt and requires no electricity to operate, it is an ideal camping companion. We have used it in the most primitive of places, where it contentedly warms itself over comfortable coals and is soon cooking meals as easily as if it were at home. Could another pan do so well, or give such flavor to morning bacon or freshly caught trout?

Not only does it lend a pioneer flair to campfire, but again it shows its versatility by doubling as a handy weapon. Any wild beast that gets bopped with this pan won't stay around long, nor be likely to return. It has, on occasion, been pressed into service to anchor the boat—and more than once has kept eager young prospectors busy for hours, panning for gold.

Mother had an iron skillet, too. She used it on a black Monarch wood range during the lean Depression years. It did more than fry potatoes. On long winter evenings, at Christmastime or New Year's Eve, it became our popcorn popper. Though it was sometimes necessary to have a small argument over whose turn it was to "shake the pan," a better corn popper has yet to be invented.

My own skillet has served me well through many happy years. When my matronly friend wrapped it lovingly in gift paper and presented it to me, she passed on a heritage of which I might never have been aware. Now my mother, and my mother's mother, and her mother before her and I have all shared one thing in common—the knowledge that with an iron skillet within easy reach, a woman can handle almost any problem.

No, my skillet needn't be disturbed by the younger, prettier pans that surround it. It's true, it can't shine or gleam or reflect the light the way they do, but it doesn't have to. It can rest on queen-size laurels, for it has bridged the generation gap between the good old days and now. ◆

### Fried Pumpkin

*This is a very old recipe. I was told by older people in this area that they fried pumpkins to take the place of meat, which was very scarce.*

1 neck pumpkin
Milk
1 egg
Salt and pepper
½ cup flour
Shortening

Get a long necked pumpkin. Peel the pumpkin and slice it very thin. Make a mixture of milk, egg, salt and pepper. After soaking the sliced pumpkin in salted water for several hours, dip the pumpkin in the mixture and roll in flour. Fry slowly in shortening until brown.

—*Mary A. Deppen*

### Batter-Fried Blossoms

Pick 1 quart of blossoms fresh. Rinse with cool water several times. Snip off green stem and dry on towel. Use 1 egg, 1 cup milk, 1 cup flour, ½ teaspoon salt, and a pinch of pepper. Roll or dip in batter and fry like white mushrooms.

If each blossom is fried separately, they will look like fried mushrooms. The taste is similar and very good.

—*Mrs. Charles B. Reeves*

# Grandma Klose's Apron

*By Lucille Howe*

Grandma Klose, a sturdy German immigrant woman, asked that she be dressed for burial in her warm winter underwear. I would have been less surprised if she had asked to wear her apron to her final resting place, for so constantly did she wear that apron that I find it almost impossible to call up a memory picture of her without it.

Of course, Grandma went apronless to church, but we attended a different congregation; and if we walked over to visit her on Sunday

afternoon, she would already have changed into everyday attire. She went without the apron, I'm sure, when she joined the family for a holiday dinner at the home of a son or daughter, but these occasions were rare and became more so as she grew older. She preferred to have us visit her. Grandma's apron was as practical and sturdy as she herself. No dainty bit of ruffles and ribbon for her. I can just hear her scornful opinion of such a one, delivered in emphatic German. The garment I remember so well was made of a couple of widths of material gathered onto a waistband, skirt fashion. It was long enough to reach the hem of her dress, which, in turn, reached her ankles, and wide enough to cover her hips. Ties sewed to the band allowed her to fasten the apron about her waist.

Up to now I have spoken of Grandma's apron in the singular, although I know, of course, that she had many. I believe the reason I think of an apron instead of several aprons is that they were always made the same, and of the same sort of materials—calico or gingham in small figures and subdued colors.

Most of us wear aprons to protect our dresses. Grandma Klose's protected, too, when she washed dishes at the kitchen table or the stove (the sink was for washing hands) or when she scrubbed clothes clean on the old washboard. But Grandma's apron was much more than a protector—oh, much, much more. It was, as needed, a chaser, a wrap, a swatter, a wiper, a fan, a carry-all.

When I remember my *grossmutter,* I am most likely to see her hurrying out the kitchen door, down the wooden steps, across the driveway to the woodpile, gathering up the hem of her apron as she goes to make a bag. This she quickly fills with split wood which she carries back to the kitchen to feed the hungry black monster, the cookstove. I wonder how many such trips a day it took.

Many other things were carried in the apron: something from the garden, eggs from a nest Grandma came across, twigs she picked up in the yard after a windstorm, bits of wood for kindling, clean cobs after she shelled corn for the chickens with the hand-cranked sheller. I'm not at all sure that chicken, ducklings and goslings did not at one time or another have an apron ride.

If some of our family walked over to visit on a summer Sunday afternoon, we would almost surely sit out on the freshly scrubbed back steps if the weather was fine. If Mother was there, the conversation would be carried on in English. But, if Mother stayed at home to rest or to see that the babies took naps, Dad and Grandma always spoke German. I knew no German, but had somehow caught on that when they used the word *madchen,* they were probably talking about me or one of my sisters, and I would get self-conscious and fidgety.

Presently Grandma would say, "Shall we go to the orchard and see if the strawberry crabs are ripe?"

Ah, those wonderful apples! I have long since learned to call them Whitneys, and they are still my favorite apples. None have ever tasted so ambrosial as the ones in that orchard. Grandma and Dad would see that each of us children had several to eat, then Grandma would fill her apron with windfalls to be used with others for jelly juice. Another day it might be cherries or plums we picked.

Back to the steps we would go, but hardly would we all be seated, when we would see Grandma jump up and go off at half-run, gathering her apron halfway up, making a chaser of it. We knew, before we spotted her, that a hen had found her way into the garden. It did not take long with Grandma swishing her chaser wildly about, and hurling a couple of clods of earth, as well as a few choice German expletives, until that hen found a way over, under or through the fence.

Errant hens were not the only creatures Grandma chased with the help of her apron. Grasping the lower corners, she would gently flutter it to guide baby chicks to shelter if a storm threatened, or if they did not go into their coops at night. She would chase a hissing gander away from a frightened child, probably me.

But what Grandma chased in the greatest numbers was—are you ready?—flies. Anyone born since insecticides came into common use can have no idea what the fly problem was like 70 years ago, especially on the farm.

Grandma baked bread regularly using good old yeast foam. She started the batter at night, wrapping the mixture with everything from blankets to buffalo coats to keep it warm. In the morning she added flour and kneaded the dough in the big pan the batter had risen in, turning and turning the pan against her tummy. Yes, it was hard on her apron, but a new apron cost less than a new dress, and a soiled apron was easier to launder than a soiled dress.

At the stove, Grandma used her apron as a pot holder to handle the hot bread pans, kettles, the oven door and the lid lifter. She also used it to fan away the heat when she opened the oven door to peek at the baking bread.

In hot weather, Grandma occasionally fanned herself with her apron, or used it to chase flies or mosquitoes. I say "occasionally" because most of the time she was too busy to let little things like bugs interfere with what she was doing. If a breeze became too cool as she rested after chores, she would throw a corner of the apron over her shoulder, or untie it and wrap it around her. Caught in a sudden shower, she would use the apron as protection for her head and shoulders.

Had Grandma worn glasses, I know what she would have used to wipe them, but I can't recall ever seeing her with any, although she read her Bible regularly.

Aunt Leonora once told me that Grandma Klose thought it was a sin to be idle. By that rule she was a saint. It was a good thing that both she and her apron were made of sturdy stuff. ◆

### Grandma's Kaffee Klatsch Bread

4 cups white flour
2 cups bran
½ cup sugar
1 teaspoon salt
2 teaspoons baking soda
2½ cups buttermilk *or* sour milk
1 egg, slightly beaten
1 cup raisins
½ cup chopped nuts (optional)
1 cup sorghum molasses
Preheat oven to 250 degrees.

Mix flour, bran, sugar and salt in a large bowl. Dissolve baking soda in buttermilk, then add to dry ingredients. Blend in remaining ingredients.

Pour into 2 greased bread pans and bake in a slow oven 1 hour and 20 minutes.

—*Mrs. Carl J. Zeitler*

## My Mother's Apron

My mother's old checkered apron
Was a garment full and wide;
It filled its humble mission,
And a million more beside....
'Twas made of 6-cent gingham,
It was neither fine nor grand,
Just a plain and simple pattern,
Made by a busy hand;
It had a little cross-stitch
Along the bottom row
And two long strings that tied behind,
In a hasty half-hitch bow.
It had no lace or ruffles,
Nor pretty appliqué,
But its simple, homey usefulness
Was an epic of the day.
'Twas used to shoo the flies,
'Twas used to wipe away the tears,
From weeping infant's eyes,
'Twas used to carry in the eggs,
In leafy bowers,
And bring in half-drowned chicks
Caught in sudden showers.
'Twas used to fill the kindling box

With chips of cobs and twigs,
And tote the pesky pursley weed
From the garden to the pigs.
'Twas used to snatch the hot kettles
When a pot rag was not at hand,
To tighten on fruit jar lids
When winter stores were canned.
'Twas used to gather garden stuff
And peaches from the hill,
And many a mess of greens
Did Mother's apron fill.
Her hands were sheltered from the gale
Beneath the sheltered fold
And tiny feet nestled there
On mornings bleak and cold.
'Twas a queenly garment
And Mother was queen,
As memory brings back to me,
'Twas a noble thing, I ween,
And when I wander at Heaven's throng,
With robes so bright and fair,
I'll say the old checkered apron
Is what I want to wear.

—*Author Unknown*

# Country Washtubs

*By Shirley Lewis Calhoun*

When I go to do my wash in this day of modern laundry—clothes washed and rinsed all in one machine—I think of my mom's washtubs. Though I have a dryer, I, like my mom, hang my clothes out on the line. My clothespins are the snap-on type. My mom used the round-top peg type, and we children used them, also—for toys. My brother used them for his cars and trucks on the dirt pile, and we girls put faces on them for our dolls. How my mom would get after us on washday, which was always on a Monday.

What I remember most were the washtubs. They were two big, black, round tubs, used for most anything. Our home was in the country, not far from a creek. We had no electricity or running water. We girls would carry those two big tubs to the creek for rinse water when Mom washed clothes. On Saturday night, the same two tubs would be filled with water for our baths; my three sisters and I took turns in the tubs.

In the summer, when Mom canned her vegetables, off again we would go to the creek and fill the tubs with water to wash the jars. Then, after filling the jars, Mom would arrange them on wooden slats which she had laid in the bottom of a clean washtub, then placed the whole thing over a fire in the back yard. This was the way she did her canning.

Come fall, I peeled plenty of apples, throwing them into the tubs to be washed before they were cooked down into apple butter. In the summer when the water was low, we had a natural spring. We also carried water in the tubs for household uses.

A few years ago, we girls got our mom a set of modern laundry tubs, which she uses on washday. She still uses the old washtubs for canning, and stores them in the basement. I know what it is like to fill lamps, wash the lamp globes, get in wood and coal, walk to meet a school bus, help Dad skin squirrels and rabbits, take cod liver oil, carry apple-butter sandwiches to school, eat my oatmeal, and go to bed when the lamp is blown out at 8 o'clock. Those days will never be again! ◆

## A Laundry "Receet" From About 1870

1. Build fire in back yard to heat kettle of rainwater.

2. Set tubs so smoke won't blow in eyes if wind is pert.

3. Shave one whole cake of lye soap in biling water.

4. Sort things. Make three piles: one pile whites, one pile colored, one pile work britches and rags.

5. Stir flour in cold water to smooth, then thin down with biling water.

6. Rub dirty spots on board, scrub hard, then bile; rub colored but don't bile; just wrench and starch.

7. Spread tea towels on grass.

8. Hand old rags on fence.

9. Pour wrench water on flower beds.

10. Scrub porch with hot, soapy water.

11. Turn tubs upside down.

12. Go put on clean dress, smooth hair with side combs, brew a cup of tea, set and rest and rock a spell, and count your blessings.

*—Author Unknown*

# The Cedar Water Bucket

By David A. Sorrel

Have you ever had a drink of water from a bucket made from the wood of a cedar tree? If not, you have missed a rare treat. Let me tell you about it.

Seventy years ago, I think I can safely say, every kitchen in our town had a cedar water bucket. And every dwelling had a well not far from the kitchen door. These were known as dug wells and went down 30–40 feet. These wells were lined with brick and produced a fine, clear, cold water.

To lift the water from the well, there had to be a pump of some sort, unless the householder was unable to afford one. In that case, a bucket on a rope that ran over a pulley was held in place by a couple of 2 by 4's that were nailed to a box around the top of the well.

Most folks in our town were able to afford a pump—either an iron pump, for those who could afford it, or a wooden pump. That was the kind we had.

All these pumps shared two characteristics. In summer they would sometimes lose their "prime," as we called it. When the prime was lost, the thing to do was pour water into the top of the pump and work the handle real fast, and most of the time the pump would start working again. Pumps also froze up in very cold weather; then a teakettle of boiling water was poured into it to thaw it out.

Besides furnishing the water we drank, the well had another useful purpose. It served as our icebox. There were only two things we tried to keep cool: butter and milk. They were placed in a tin bucket and let down close to the cool water.

A watermelon was different; they were too big for a bucket. So we filled a washtub with the cold water and put the melon in it to chill.

Our kitchen had a dining table where we ate our meals. And there was the wooden cupboard where Mother kept her clean tablecloths, dish towels and so on.

Another thing in this old cupboard greatly attracted me. This was a cob pipe and a paper sack of dried mullein leaves. Smoking these leaves in a pipe was thought to be a fine remedy for catarrh (I think we call it "sinus" now). One day when there was no one around to stop me, I tried this remedy. I don't recall that it made me ill, but the smoke had a vile taste.

Just on the other side of the cupboard was what we called the safe, perhaps 6 feet tall, 18 inches deep and 4 feet wide. On the bottom shelves we stored leftover food. The top shelves were used to hold the company dishes.

In a drawer that ran the full length of the safe we kept our knives and forks. We were not affluent enough to afford the silver kind. Ours had black wooden handles, and the forks had only three tines.

Across from the safe was the cookstove, a cast-iron range. Building a fire in this stove could only be accomplished by practice and experience.

Beside the stove was the cob box. In summer it was my job to keep the cob box filled. In winter I was supposed to fill two buckets with coal and set them right by the stove.

Next to the stove stood the table that held our cedar water bucket. The bucket was made from red cedar wood and was bound with three shining brass hoops. It held about 2 gallons of water and a tin dipper.

Coming to this bucket of water on a hot day when I was very hot and thirsty, I plunged the dipper deep into the water and drank from it. As I savored the clear, cool water I had craved so greatly, I could smell and taste the sweet flavor that the cedar wood gave to the water. Again I dipped and drank, and it was cool, sweet and satisfying to a thirsty boy.

Seventy years later, as I drink the chloride-filled water that comes from a faucet in our kitchen, my mind goes back to the old cedar water bucket and the good water that it held for a thirsty boy. ◆

# The Coffee Grinder

### By Marie Anderson

There it was, the coffee grinder, back on the little old farm, perched way up on top of the warming oven of the stove.

Mom would say to me, "Marie, take down the coffee grinder and grind some coffee. Mrs. Erickson is coming over." She poured the coffee beans into the little place on top of the grinder (she never measured), and I sat on that old kitchen chair with the grinder between my knees, grinding away. What a lovely humming sound—and what an aroma. That coffee was fresh, believe me. Peabody Coffee, yes, that was the name.

And there, on the old wood-burning stove, stood the white enamel coffeepot, with water boiling. Mom pulled out the drawer from the grinder and dumped the coffee into the pot while I scrounged the floor, finding the few beans that had bounced out while I was grinding.

When Mrs. Erickson came, coffee was served, and Mmmm! That was good coffee! I got a taste, too, even though I was just a little girl.

Later we got a grinder with a sliding cover over the beans. Now that was really something. The beans didn't jump out any more.

Coffee always came in paper bags, never in tin cans. The grinder had a screw for setting your own choice of coarseness and Mom knew just how to set it to brew the best coffee. Oh yes, she was a master coffee maker! ◆

# The Old Kitchen Floor

Far back in my youth my thoughts have been cast
To the house where the hours of my childhood
 passed;
I loved all its rooms, to the pantry and hall,
But the blessed old kitchen was dearer than all.

Its chairs and its table, none brighter could be,
And all its surroundings were sacred to me,
To the nails in the ceiling, the latch on the door,
And I loved every crack in the old kitchen floor.

The grand old stone fireplace, with mouth high
 and wide,
The old-fashioned fireplace that stood by its side,
From which came so often the puddings and pies
That fairly bewildered and dazzled our eyes.

Here, too, good St. Nicholas, crafty and still,
Came down every Christmas our stockings to fill;
But the sweetest memories laid up in store
Are of Mother, who trod on the old kitchen floor.

Day in and day out, from morning till night,
Her footsteps were busy, her heart always light;

Oh, it seemed to me then that she knew not a care,
The smile was so kindly her face used to wear.

I remember so plainly what joy filled our eyes
When she told us the stories that children so
 prize;
They were new every night, though we'd heard
 them before
From her lips, by the wheel on the old kitchen
 floor.

Tonight those old visions come back at their will,
Though the wheel and the music forever are still;
The spindle is broken, the wheel laid away,
And the dear hands that turned it have moldered
 to clay.

The hearthstone, so sacred, is just as 'twas then,
And the voices of children ring out there again;
The sun through the windows shines in as of yore,
But strange feet are treading the old kitchen floor.

—*Author Unknown*